Rights
and Wrongs

Rights and Wrongs

Women's Struggle for Legal Equality

SECOND EDITION

Susan Cary Nicholas
Alice M. Price
Rachel Rubin

WOMEN'S LAW PROJECT / PHILADELPHIA

Revised and updated by Alice M. Price

The Feminist Press
at The City University of New York

NEW YORK

**Library of Congress
Cataloging-in-Publication Data**

Nicholas, Susan Cary.
  Rights and Wrongs.

  (Women's lives, women's work)
  Includes bibliographical references and index.
  1. Women—Legal status, laws, etc.—United
States. I. Price, Alice M. II. Rubin, Rachel. III.
Title.
KF478.N53 1986   346.7301'34   86-2461
ISBN 0-935312-42-0   347.306134

Cover photo: The Bettmann Archive

Table of Contents

Striving for First-class Citizenship

Early Struggles for Equality • A Distinguished Law-breaker •
Glued to the Pedestal • The Nineteenth Amendment •
Problems of Protective Legislation • Recent Advances toward
Equality • Discrimination in the Military • The Equal Rights
Amendment: Writing Women into the Constitution

The Three Unequal Partners

Similarities between Marriage and Business Contracts •
Ignorance Is the Rule • State Laws Define the Terms •
Traditional Definitions of Marriage • Effects of the "Merger of
Identities" Theory • Married Women's Property Acts • What's
in a Name? • Obligations Imposed by Traditional Marriage
Law • Position of the Homemaker Wife • Court Refuses
to Interfere • Mrs. Hardy's Allowance • Mrs. Glover's
Misbehavior • Experiments in Redefining Marriage • Some
Early Dissenters • New Marriage Contracts • Will the Courts
Go Along? • The Community Property System • The
Uniform Marriage and Divorce Act • A New View of Alimony •
"No-fault" Divorce • Child Custody: A Step Forward • Positive
Effects of State ERAs

Injustice in the Marketplace

The Trials and the Satisfactions • "Ma" Bell's History of
Discrimination • A Woman's Place: Low- or No-paying Jobs •

The Question of "Protection" • Antidiscrimination Laws and
Remedies • AT&T: An Unprecedented Victory • When Is a
BFOQ Not a BFOQ? • When Is a "Neutral Rule" Not Neutral? •
The "Business Necessity" Test • Affirmative Action Policy •
Some Thorny Problems • Progress Has Been Slow • Special
Issues Related to Insurance • What the Future Holds

61   FOUR: Women and Their Bodies
The Right to Control

Rape • The Two Faces of Eve: A Cherished Stereotype •
The Victim As Criminal • Steps toward Reform • The Right to
Choose Parenthood • "Woman's Biological Servitude to Man" •
The Intrepid Margaret Sanger • A Less-than-perfect Victory •
The Shift in Public Opinion • Woman-killers: The Antiabortion
Laws • A Woman's Constitutional Right to Decide • Rights
Remain in Peril • Low-income Women: "Let Them Eat
Cake" • Some Unanswered Questions

Publisher's Acknowledgments

EARLY IN 1973, Mariam Chamberlain and Terry Saario of the Ford Foundation spent one day visiting The Feminist Press on the campus of the State University of New York / College at Old Westbury. They heard staff members describe the early history of The Feminist Press and its goal—to change the sexist education of girls and boys, women and men, through publishing and other projects. They also heard about those books and projects then in progress; they felt our sense of frustration about how little we were able to do directly for the classroom teacher. Advising us about funding, Terry Saario was provocative. "You need to think of yourselves," she said, "in the manner of language labs, testing and developing new texts for students and new instructional materials for teachers." Our "language" was feminism, our intent to provide alternatives to the sexist texts used in schools. The conception was, in fact, precisely the one on which the Press had been founded.

Out of that 1973 meeting came the idea for the *Women's Lives / Women's Work* project. This project, which would not officially begin for more than two years, has allowed us to extend the original concept of The Feminist Press to a broader audience.

In the summer of 1975, the final proposal—to produce for copublication a series of twelve supplementary books and their accompanying teaching guides—was funded by the Ford Foundation and the Carnegie Corporation. Project officers Terry Saario and Vivien Stewart were supportive and helpful throughout the life of the project.

Once funding was obtained, The Feminist Press began its search for additional staff to work on the project. The small nucleus of existing staff working on the project was expanded as The Feminist Press hired new employees. The *Women's Lives / Women's Work* project staff ultimately included eight people who remained for the duration of the project: Sue Davidson, Shirley Frank, Merle Froschl, Florence Howe, Mary Mulrooney, Elizabeth Phillips, Susan Trowbridge, and Sandy Weinbaum. Two other people, Dora Janeway Odarenko and Michele Russell, were on the staff through 1977, and we wish to acknowledge their contributions. Helen Schrader, a Feminist Press staff member, participated on the project during its first year and kept financial records and wrote financial reports throughout the duration of the project.

The *Women's Lives / Women's Work* project staff adopted the methods of work and the decision-making structure developed by The

Feminist Press staff as a whole. As a Press "work committee," the project met weekly to make decisions, review progress, discuss problems. The project staff refined the editorial direction of the project, conceptualized and devised guidelines for the books, and identified prospective authors. When proposals came in, the project staff read and evaluated the submissions, and made decisions regarding them. Similarly, when manuscripts arrived, the project staff read and commented on them. Project staff members took turns drafting memoranda, reports, and other documents. And the design of the series grew out of the discussions and the ideas generated at the project meetings. The books, teaching guides, and other informational materials had the advantage, at significant stages of development, of the committee's collective direction.

The process of evaluation by teachers and students before final publication was as important as the process for developing ideas into books. To this end, we produced testing editions of the books. Field-testing networks were set up throughout the United States in a variety of schools—public, private, inner-city, small town, suburban, and rural—to reach as diverse a student population as possible. We field tested in the following cities, regions, and states: Boston, Massachusetts; Tucson, Arizona; Seattle, Washington; Los Angeles, California; Tampa, Florida; Greensboro, North Carolina; Eugene, Oregon; Martha's Vineyard, Massachusetts; New York City; Long Island; New Jersey; Rhode Island. We also had an extensive network of educators —350 teachers across the country—who reviewed the books in the series, often using sections of books in classrooms. From teachers' comments, from students' questionnaires, and from tapes of teachers' discussions, we gained valuable information both for revising the books and for developing the teaching guides.

We would like to thank the following people with whom we consulted about *Rights and Wrongs: Women's Struggle for Legal Equality.* David J. Danelski, Department of Government, Cornell University; Elizabeth F. Defeis, School of Law, Seton Hall University; Judith R. Gething, Department of American Studies, University of Hawaii / Manoa; Ruth Bader Ginsburg, School of Law, Columbia University; James W. Hauser, Bellevue High School, Bellevue, Washington; Bertha R. S. Houser, Attorney at Law, Seattle, Washington; Kate A. Hunter, Seattle, Washington; Deborah P. Kelly, Department of Political Science, Johns Hopkins University; Merle Levine, Wheatley High School, East Williston, New York; Mary McAulay, John F. Kennedy High School, Bronx, New York; Eleanor Newirth, John F. Kennedy

High School, Plainview, New York; Janice B. Snook, Department of Political Science, University of South Florida / Tampa; Lawrence Tannenbaum, Hewlett High School, Lynbrook, New York.

Three times during the life of the *Women's Lives / Women's Work* project, an Advisory Board composed of feminist educators and scholars met for a full day to discuss the books and teaching guides. The valuable criticisms and suggestions of the following people who participated in these meetings were essential to the project: Millie Alpern, Rosalyn Baxandall, Peggy Brick, Ellen Cantarow, Elizabeth Ewen, Barbara Gates, Clarisse Gillcrist, Elaine Hedges, Nancy Hoffman, Susan Klaw, Alice Kessler-Harris, Roberta Kronberger, Merle Levine, Eleanor Newirth, Judith Oksner, Naomi Rosenthal, Judith Schwartz, Judy Scott, Carroll Smith-Rosenberg, Adria Steinberg, Barbara Sussman, Amy Swerdlow. We also want to express our gratitude to Shirley McCune and Nida Thomas, who acted in a general advisory capacity and made many useful suggestions; and to Kathryn Girard and Kathy Salisbury who helped to develop the teacher and student field-testing questionnaires.

THE FEMINIST PRESS

Authors' Acknowledgments

THE AUTHORS would like to acknowledge and thank the founders of the Women's Law Project, Barbara Brown, Ann Freedman, and Harriet Katz, who have served as our mentors over the years and who, both individually and collectively, produced much of the original research and many of the theories regarding women's legal rights which appear in this book.

Publisher's Preface to the Second Edition

WRITTEN IN 1976 AND 1977 by one of the first feminist law collectives, the first edition of *Rights and Wrongs* reached readers in October 1978. It represented an early attempt to tell the story of the current feminist battles for legal rights to a large school, college, and general audience eager for the news. The eagerness, moreover, included a new appreciation—growing out of women's studies—for the history of these legal battles. Thus, the context of each chapter in the volume was historical, and even the arrangement of chapters, from Constitutional rights to the newest—the rights of women with regard to their own bodies—was historical. This first edition went through several printings by 1982, when the demise of the Equal Rights Amendment led to the decision to revise the volume rather than reprint it.

In the decade since work was first begun on *Rights and Wrongs*, the consciousness of both women and men has grown clearer about the urgency and necessity for these legal questions to be understood in a world in which they will continue to be debated. In the past decade, the changing political atmosphere and the continual testing and interpreting of the Constitution in the courts have brought both advances and setbacks to the legal status of women. The most radical loss was the Equal Rights Amendment. The new text includes the failure of passage in 1982 and the subsequent re-introduction of the amendment into Congress.

Perhaps the most remarkable difference in women's condition over the past decade reflected in this new edition is the alarming rise in reported incidents of sexual harassment and domestic violence. The term "sexual harassment" was not even in common use until after 1980. New in this volume is a discussion of the growing problem of domestic violence and the responses of both the legal system and women's support networks to the needs of victims.

Other key areas have been affected by the developments of the past decade. The Supreme Court's stance regarding sex-based discrimination, analyzed here through cases heard in 1981 and 1984, has been that the Court is willing to uphold sex-based discrimination in some cases (for example, in draft registration), though not in others. In divorce law, the courts are deciding in favor of joint custody more often than before, and paying more attention thus to the needs of children in such cases.

The area of employment has continued to be the scene of women's legal battles. Affirmative action has been both helped and hindered by Court decisions in various cases since 1977. Two major trends have emerged regarding women and work. First, the feminization of poverty—especially for women of color—has brought sharpened attention to the continuing, shocking disparity between the incomes of men and women. Second, this sharpened apprehension, coupled with the intransigence of the sexual division of the labor force, has led to a new effort to gain, not "equal pay for equal work," but rather, equal pay for work of "comparable worth." The concept of pay equity has begun a new series of legal battles reported on here.

Further, legal gains have been made for women in some areas in insurance benefits, pensions, and for pregnancy-related conditions. Finally, with regard to the areas affecting women's bodies, controversies continue to rage over legalized abortion and contraception, as well as the newer area of pornography.

As we go to press in the mid-eighties, we are conscious that this new edition will serve not only thousands of readers in the United States, many of whom were children a decade ago, but also an increasingly sharp feminist consciousness around the world. Indian, Japanese, Latin American, Caribbean, African, and European feminists are curious about the legal battles of women in the United States. How and why have some of women's legal problems worsened? Why is it that both Canada and India can boast of an ERA, while the United States cannot? This edition takes these questions to the current moment.

Introduction

THIS IS A BOOK about a movement as old as our nation, the ongoing battle of women to gain the right to participate in and contribute to society as full and equal citizens. Four major areas of concern to women—constitutional law, the family, employment, and the right to control over their bodies—will be covered. In looking at each, we will examine some of the many ways in which women have been excluded from the mainstream of our culture, how their lives have been limited, and how, through continuing efforts, they have advanced step by step toward the goal of equality.

In each chapter we will be looking at the world from the special perspective of the law. To many readers, this perspective may be unfamiliar, since most of us tend to believe that the law is for lawyers only and does not concern either our daily lives or the course of history. Yet the law has always been a focal point of the movement for women's rights. As you will see in reading the following chapters, it has often been a conservative force, perpetuating the subordinate status of women. At other times in our history, the law has played a progressive part in creating new rights for women.

At the Nation's Founding

As early as 1776, Abigail Adams accurately perceived the crucial importance of the law in governing the lives of women. In a letter to her husband, John Adams, she attempted to impress upon him the necessity of correcting historical injustices toward women while the new government was being formed:

> . . . in the new Code of Laws which I suppose it will be necessary for you to make I desire you would Remember the Ladies, and be more generous and favourable to them than your ancestors. Do not put such unlimited power into the hands of the Husbands. Remember all Men would be tyrants if they could. If perticuliar care and attention is not paid to the Laidies we are determined to foment a Rebelion, and will not hold ourselves bound by any Laws in which we have no voice, or Representation.[1]

Unfortunately, the founding fathers did not take Abigail Adams's warning seriously. The Constitution they eventually adopted left the old legal injustices intact, and by the middle of the nineteenth century, Abigail Adams's prediction of rebellion was becoming less fanciful. In 1848, the first women's rights convention, called by Lucretia Mott and Elizabeth Cady Stanton, took place in Seneca Falls, New York. Designed to discuss "the social, civil, and religious rights of women," the convention was attended by approximately three hundred women and men. Seneca Falls marked the beginning of a long, difficult, often bitter struggle to win equal rights for women.

The Declaration of Sentiments

Like Abigail Adams seventy-two years before, the women and men at Seneca Falls understood the ways in which the law oppressed women. The convention's Declaration of Sentiments, patterned after the Declaration of Independence, focused on the legal inequities faced by women at that time:

DECLARATION OF SENTIMENTS. When, in the course of human events, it becomes necessary for one portion of the family of man to assume among the people of the earth a position different from that which they have hitherto occupied, but one to which the laws of nature and of nature's God entitle them, a decent respect to the opinions of mankind requires that they should declare the causes that impel them to such a course.

We hold these truths to be self-evident: that all men and women are created equal; that they are endowed by their Creator with certain inalienable rights; that among these are life, liberty, and the pursuit of happiness; that to secure these rights governments are instituted, deriving their just powers from the consent of the governed. Whenever any form of government becomes destructive of these ends, it is the right of those who suffer from it to refuse allegiance to it, and to insist upon the institution of a new government, laying its foundation on such principles, and organizing its powers in such form, as to them shall seem most likely to effect their safety and happiness. Prudence, indeed, will dictate that governments long established should not be changed for light and transient causes; and accordingly all experience hath shown that mankind are more disposed to suffer, while evils are sufferable, than to right themselves by abolishing the forms to which they were accustomed. But when a long train of abuses and usurpations, pursuing invariably the same object, evinces a design to reduce them under absolute despotism, it is their duty to throw off such government, and to provide new guards for their future security. Such has been the patient sufferance of the women under this government, and such is now the necessity which constrains them to demand the equal station to which they are entitled.

The history of mankind is a history of repeated injuries and usurpations on the part of man toward woman, having in direct object the establishment of an absolute tyranny over her. To prove this, let facts be submitted to a candid world.

He has never permitted her to exercise her inalienable right to the elective franchise.

He has compelled her to submit to laws, in the formation of which she had no voice.

He has withheld from her rights which are given to the most ignorant and degraded men—both natives and foreigners.

Having deprived her of this first right of a citizen, the elective franchise, thereby leaving her without representation in the halls of legislation, he has oppressed her on all sides.

He has made her, if married, in the eye of the law, civilly dead.

He has taken from her all right in property, even to the wages she earns.

He has made her, morally, an irresponsible being, as she can commit many crimes with impunity, provided they be done in the presence of her husband. In the covenant of marriage, she is compelled to promise obedience to her husband, he becoming, to all intents and purposes, her master—the law giving him power to deprive her of her liberty, and to administer chastisement.

He has so framed the laws of divorce, as to what shall be the proper causes, and in case of separation, to whom the guardianship of the children shall be given, as to be wholly regardless of the happiness of women—the law, in all cases, going upon the false supposition of the supremacy of man, and giving all power into his hands.

After depriving her of all rights as a married woman, if single, and the owner of property, he has taxed her to support a government which recognizes her only when her property can be made profitable to it.

He has monopolized nearly all the profitable employments, and from those she is permitted to follow, she receives but a scanty remuneration. He closes against her all the avenues to wealth and distinction which he considers most honorable to himself. As a teacher of theology, medicine, or law, she is not known.

He has denied her the facilities for obtaining a thorough education, all colleges being closed against her.

He allows her in Church, as well as State, but a subordinate position, claiming Apostolic authority for her exclusion from the ministry, and, with some exceptions, from any public participation in the affairs of the Church.

He has created a false public sentiment by giving to the world a different code of morals for men and women, by which moral delinquencies which exclude women from society, are not only tolerated, but deemed of little account in man.

He has usurped the prerogative of Jehovah himself, claiming it as his right to assign for her a sphere of action, when that belongs to her conscience and to her God.

He has endeavored, in every way that he could, to destroy her confidence in her own powers, to lessen her self-respect, and to make her willing to lead a dependent and abject life.

Now, in view of this entire disfranchisement of one-half the people of this country, their social and religious degradation—in view of the unjust laws above mentioned, and because women do feel themselves aggrieved, oppressed, and fraudulently deprived of their most sacred rights, we insist that they have immediate admission to all the rights and privileges which belong to them as citizens of the United States.[2]

Obviously, many of the repressive laws of 1848 no longer exist, but there remain innumerable ways in which the legal system affects women and the movement for equality. We hope in this book to develop an awareness of the impact of the law on our daily lives: to show how it regulates matters as personal as our names and our marriages; how it shapes and is shaped by societal attitudes; and how it can be used, by those who understand it, to forward or to impede social change.

A System of Federalism

In order to use the law effectively, it is important to understand in general terms how the legal system operates. Like our government as a whole, the law is a system of federalism. Certain powers are given to the federal government, with the remainder being left for the individual states to handle. In the area of law commonly called "civil rights," the federal government has traditionally carried the bulk of the responsibility for setting policy and seeing that the law is enforced. Thus, women's legal rights are frequently established first at the federal level, through decisions of the United States Supreme Court or acts of Congress prohibiting discrimination. In this way a national standard is developed which, over time, filters down to the local level of enforcement.

On the other hand, some areas of law are generally governed by the individual states. One of the most important of these for women concerns laws relating to the family, marriage, and divorce. These laws often vary from state to state. For example, the answer to a woman's question about whether she would be given half the family assets in the event of divorce differs depending on whether she lives in Pennsylvania or Texas. By contrast, a woman's right to be free of sex discrimination in employment remains constant, regardless of where she happens to live, because equal employment opportunity is largely a matter of federal law.

What Is the "Law"?

Both the state and federal legal systems embody a complex hierarchy of different kinds of law, emanating from different sources. In order to know what the "law" is, one must go beyond the statute books and become familiar with the ways in which the laws are applied by the courts, and, to a lesser extent, by government agencies. Legislation, regulations, and court opinions together create a particular legal status for women at each stage in our history; the "law" is by necessity a combination of all these sources of policy.

The highest authority within this hierarchy of law is the United States Constitution. Every other kind of state or federal law must be in accord with this fundamental charter of our government. The Constitution establishes the structure of our government, consisting of the executive, the legislative, and the judicial branches. These three branches are designed to be equal, and the Constitution sets out an intricate mechanism of checks and balances in order to preserve this equality. It also governs the relationship between the state and federal systems. In this book we will be most concerned with the relationship between the legislative and judicial branches of government: how the legislature and the courts act together to form the laws which govern us.

In addition to setting forth the structure of government, the Constitution enumerates certain basic rights of all persons, such as the right to free speech and the right to equal protection of the law. As you will read in the chapter on constitutional law, the right to equal protection has become extremely important in the development of women's legal rights.

The legislative branch of government, represented by Congress on the federal level, is invested with the basic lawmaking power of passing statutes setting out the public policy of the country. An example of a congressional enactment of importance to women is the Equal Pay Act, requiring employers to afford equal pay for equal work, regardless of the sex of the employee.

The judicial branch—the United States Supreme Court and the lower federal courts—has the responsibility for interpreting legislative enactments and applying them to the facts of individual cases. Thus, a female employee, believing herself to be receiving lower wages than men for doing the same job, would seek relief in the federal courts under the Equal Pay Act. In deciding her case, the court would analyze all the relevant data about her situation, including her job description, that of men doing equivalent work, and the company's pay scale. Based on this evidence, the court would then decide whether Congress intended the Equal Pay Act to prohibit the kind of behavior practiced by her employer.

As well as resolving individual disputes, court decisions become precedent which lower courts are required to follow in considering similar cases. In this way, a body of law known as "case law" is slowly built up which gives more definite meaning to the general language of statutes. A similar process takes place in areas of the law where no statutes have been enacted. Here the gradual accumulation of case law is known as the "common law," and consists of court-made doctrines, handed down sometimes from as early as medieval times. Many legal rules concerning the law of the family are derived from common law sources.

Among their interpretive functions, the courts have the special duty to decide when the legislature has passed a law which goes beyond the acceptable bounds articulated in the Constitution. In most instances, as we have seen, courts are bound by the will of the legislature; their duty is to decide what the legislature intended, not to substitute their own judgments about public policy. However, when a statute violates the Constitution, the court must override the legislature and invalidate that statute. During the last decade, the courts have decided that many statutes treating men and women differently conflict with the Constitution, and have invalidated the sex classification.

In recent times, governmental agencies have assumed increasing importance within our legal system. Almost every governmental agency, from the Social Security Administration to the Passport Office, has regulations which can significantly affect women's legal status. As the bodies responsible for implementing public policy on a day-to-day basis, agencies are the most visible source of law, with the most continuous impact on our daily lives. In fact, many citizens during their lives never come into contact with any source of law other than governmental agencies.

Most agencies are established under the auspices of either the executive or the legislative branch for the purpose of administering complicated governmental functions. For example, each state has a sizable department to regulate the operation and registration of motor vehicles. Sometimes governmental agencies act in a legislative manner by publishing regulations which explain and carry out legislative enactments. The federal Department of Education, for example, has been mandated by Congress to adopt regulations governing sex discrimination in schools. In addition, Congress has empowered this department to exercise a "quasi-judicial" function by granting it authority to receive complaints and decide on a case-by-case basis whether a particular situation violated Congress's prohibition against sex discrimination. However, since government agencies rank below both the courts and the legislature in the legal hierarchy, agency regulations and decisions are subject to review by the courts to determine whether they accurately reflect congressional intention and whether they comport with the Constitution.

A Dynamic System

As this brief discussion indicates, courts, legislatures, and governmental agencies intersect one another and build upon one another in a process of continual growth. It is this combination of—and often tension among—the various sources of the law which results in a legal system that is a dynamic, ever-changing institution, rather than the fixed, static documents many of us imagine when we hear the word "law."

The law is dynamic also in the sense that it reflects the values of society—or at least those of a majority of the people—as expressed through elected and appointed representatives. Sometimes, however, the law lags behind changes that have taken place in social attitudes, because the process of legal evolution is cumbersome and slow. Many of our laws relating to the family, for example, seem both out-of-date and contrary to the interests of women. At other times, the law moves far ahead of public opinion and actually helps to shape and change societal attitudes, as with federal law prohibiting sex discrimination in employment. Occasionally, the law may even create social or political backlash through its advances, as may have been the case with the Supreme Court's early abortion decision.

While public opinion can vitally affect laws relating to women, public opinion alone does not shape the laws. An effective understanding of the legal status of women requires the knowledge that legal systems, like other governmental functions, are responsive primarily to those who hold positions of power. The women at Seneca Falls realized that the laws oppressing women would never really change until women had a chance to participate in the lawmaking process. It was for this reason that the feminist movement of the nineteenth and early twentieth centuries concentrated most of its energy on gaining the right to vote.

Voting Is Not Enough

Today, however, women know that voting, by itself, will not change their condition. Recent dramatic changes in the legal status of women have come about only because of intense, sustained pressure by feminists on the legal system—through court challenges to antiquated laws and through constant demands for legislative reform. To effect these changes, women have had to educate themselves about how the legal system influences their private lives, how it operates, and how it can be changed. In increasing numbers, women have begun to seek more control over, and more responsibility for, their own lives, by organizing and by learning from women's studies and community law classes how the legal system affects them. Also, women are at last gaining greater access to the legal system by attending law schools in ever larger numbers, getting elected to Congress and state legislatures, and getting appointed as judges and agency heads.

The enrollment of women in law schools has grown dramatically since 1950 from 3.5 percent of the total school population to almost 38 percent by 1984. The 1980s have also seen the appointment of Sandra Day O'Connor as the first female justice of the United States Supreme Court, as well as the campaign of Geraldine Ferraro for Vice President of the United States. But women still remain sorely underrepresented in the more powerful positions of our federal and state governments. Our hope is that this book will show not only how far women have come, but also how far they still have to go to achieve legal equality.

Rights
and Wrongs

ONE: Women and the Constitution

Striving for First-class Citizenship

A RALLYING POINT of the struggle for sex equality in almost every generation has been the United States Constitution. As the basic charter of our government and the primary source of the rights of inhabitants, this single legal document has received more attention from advocates of women's rights than all other laws combined. The Constitution's guarantees—or lack of guarantees—for women have been the touchstones for determining their legal and political status in society.

When the Constitution was originally drafted, women had a legal status not unlike that of children and slaves. While the Constitution itself made no reference to male or female, women remained excluded from the voting process and from other participation in public affairs for well over a century after the Constitution was adopted. In fact, the movement for the emancipation of slaves gained constitutional recognition of equality for black males long before women began to gain equivalent rights of citizenship, such as the vote.

Early Struggles for Equality

During the first half of the nineteenth century, the feminist movement and the abolitionist movement shared many leaders —men and women who were concerned with the government's degradation of human worth and dignity in any form, be it the brand of slavery upon black men and women or the demeaning subordinate status in which all women were placed. Many of the leading feminists of the nineteenth century gained their first public speaking experience on the platforms of antislavery rallies. Likewise, some antislavery leaders participated in the early conventions of the women's movement.

Ironically, the original inspiration for the first women's rights convention grew out of sexist treatment of women within the antislavery movement itself—at a World Anti-Slavery Convention in London in 1840. Lucretia Mott and Elizabeth Cady Stanton, both antislavery activists, had traveled to the convention as part of the American delegation. Once there, however, they were refused admission to the main floor of the convention hall and were sent to a special gallery for women only. This treatment was a rude shock. How could they, as "free" women, help to bring an end to the slavery of black people, if they themselves were not taken seriously? The two women returned to the United States to continue their antislavery work, but also to ponder the condition of women. By 1848, they had organized the first women's rights convention at Seneca Falls, New York, and had authored the powerful Declaration of Sentiments, which recited all the most egregious forms of the oppression of women. Two major topics addressed by the Seneca Falls Convention, the right to vote and the right to pursue all occupations on an equal footing with men, soon became the focus of the women's rights movement. Most of the constitutional battles of the next seventy-five years centered around one or the other of these two fundamental rights.

A major setback for the early leaders of the women's movement came on the heels of the Civil War. Despite the ties between the women's rights and antislavery movements, national sentiment toward the "woman question" had not yet reached the high emotional pitch to which the war had raised the issues of slavery. At the end of the Civil War, the political climate favoring constitutional recognition of blacks resulted in the Thirteenth, Fourteenth, and Fifteenth Amendments to the Constitution. These amendments specifically abolished slavery, extended voting rights to black citizens, and, for the first time, spoke of citizens' rights to "equal protection of the law." It was clear at the time these amendments were passed, however, that Congress did not intend for women—black or white—to enjoy this broad grant of citizenship along with former male slaves. Concerted efforts by feminists to have women expressly included in these amendments failed, and many feminist leaders were embittered at the abandonment of their cause by those same male politicians beside whom they had fought to end slavery. Thus, while it took several more generations of struggle before black American males began to realize the promise of those new amendments, even the symbolic victory of constitutional recognition was denied to black and white women at this important juncture of history. And this victory has continued to elude women, as the struggle to secure an Equal Rights Amendment in our own time shows.

The Fourteenth Amendment, adopted in 1868, provides in its first section: "No State shall make or enforce any law which shall abridge the privileges or immunities of citizens of the United States; nor shall any State deprive any person of life, liberty, or property, without due process of law; nor deny to any person within its jurisdiction the equal protection of the laws." While the language of the amendment seems to apply equally to all persons, regardless of sex, Congress did not intend for women to be included in this grant of equality. Indeed, in the second section of the amendment, which specifies the number of representatives each state should have in Congress, the word "male" was used to describe citizens of voting age. Since this was the first time "male" had been expressly used in the Constitution, the wording drove home the exclusion of women. Two years later, when adoption of the Fifteenth Amendment guaranteed to former male slaves the right to vote, women were again passed over, despite efforts by leaders of the feminist movement to have the word "sex" added to that amendment, along with "race, color, or previous condition of servitude."

Having been abandoned by Congress, feminists in the last half of the nineteenth century were left with one other option: to seek their rights of citizenship directly from the courts. One of the first women to do so was Myra Colby Bradwell. Bradwell was a woman with a long history of political activity. Married to a lawyer, Bradwell had for many years studied law with her husband. In 1868, she began publishing her own weekly legal newspaper, the *Chicago Legal News*. The newspaper quickly became a leading legal publication, and Bradwell was recognized as one of the foremost commentators and collectors of legal opinions and legislation in her part of the country. She was active in urging passage of new legislation in such varied areas as zoning and the regulation of industry and courtroom procedures, and was an ardent supporter of equal rights for women, particularly suffrage and the right of married women to be free to manage their own property and run their own businesses. In 1869, Bradwell passed the bar examination in Illinois and applied to become a lawyer in that state. The Illinois Supreme Court denied her application because she was a woman.

Not one to be easily turned aside, Bradwell took her case to the Supreme Court of the United States, arguing that it was unconstitutional under the Fourteenth Amendment for a whole class of citizens—namely, women—to be prevented from becoming lawyers. While it was reasonable for Illinois to set standards for the education and moral character of its lawyers, she argued, it was not fair for the state to impose an arbitrary qualification which neither she nor any other woman could ever meet: being a man.

The justices of the United States Supreme Court did not agree. In their view, Illinois had a perfect right to exclude women from practicing law if it chose to do so. They saw nothing in the Fourteenth Amendment to protect against this form of exclusion. In a concurring opinion, Justice Bradley wrote:

It certainly cannot be affirmed, as an historical fact, that [the right to engage in any and every profession] has ever been established as one of the fundamental privileges and immunities of the sex. On the contrary, the civil law, as well as nature herself, has always recognized a wide difference in the respective spheres and destinies of man and woman. Man is, or should be, woman's protector and defender. The natural and proper timidity and delicacy which belongs [sic] to the female sex evidently unfits it for many of the occupations of civil life. The constitution of the family organization, which is founded in the divine ordinance, as well as in the nature of things, indicates the domestic sphere as that which properly belongs to the domain and functions of womanhood. The harmony, not to say identity, of interests and views which belong, or should belong, to the family institution is repugnant to the idea of a woman adopting a distinct and independent career from that of her husband. . . .

It is true that many women are unmarried and not affected by any of the duties, complications, and incapacities arising out of the married state, but these are exceptions to the general rule. The paramount destiny and mission of woman are to fulfil the noble and benign offices of wife and mother. This is the law of the Creator. And the rules of civil society must be adapted to the general constitution of things, and cannot be based upon exceptional cases.

The humane movements of modern society, which have for their object the multiplication of avenues for woman's advancement, and of occupations adapted to her condition and sex, have my heartiest concurrence. But I am not prepared to say that it is one of her fundamental rights and privileges to be admitted into every office and position, including those which require highly special qualifications and demanding special responsibilities.[1]

Clearly, the Court was a long way from recognizing that women, even women like Bradwell, who had excelled in a self-made career, could ever be the equals of men. As you will see in the chapter on employment, this stereotypical view that the "natural" role of women should necessarily exclude them from public life and professions has been slow in dying; women like Bradwell have been forced to return to the courts many times to champion the cause of equal employment rights for women. One perhaps cheering footnote to Bradwell's life, however, is that her petition for admission to the bar of Illinois was finally accepted twenty years later, shortly before her death; and her own daughter went on to become a practicing lawyer.

A Distinguished Law-breaker

Women's struggle to get the right to vote fared as badly in the courts during the late nineteenth century as did the fight for employment opportunity. In 1873, the year Bradwell's case came before the Supreme Court, another famous advocate of women's rights found herself in court as well—but this time as a defendant against criminal charges. The federal crime with which Susan B. Anthony and her companions were charged was that of "having voted without the lawful right to vote."[2] Anthony, along with many other women, believed that the only way for women to gain suffrage was to claim that right at the polls. To them voting was a fundamental right of citizenship, and the general language of the Fourteenth Amendment extended equally to women and men.

Anthony was found guilty of breaking the law at a trial at which she was not allowed to speak. The following day at sentencing, when at last the judge asked if she had anything to say, she responded with an angry, eloquent speech:

Miss Anthony: Yes, your honor, I have many things to say; for in your ordered verdict of guilty, you have trampled under foot every vital principle of our government. My natural rights, my civil rights, my political rights, my judicial rights, are all alike ignored. Robbed of the fundamental privilege of citizenship, I am degraded from the status of a citizen to that of a subject; and not only myself individually, but all of my sex, are, by your honor's verdict, doomed to political subjection under this, so-called, form of government.
Judge Hunt: The Court cannot listen to a rehearsal of arguments the prisoner's counsel has already consumed three hours in presenting.
Miss Anthony: May it please your honor, I am not arguing the question, but simply stating the reasons why sentence cannot, in justice, be pronounced against me. Your denial of my citizen's right to vote, is the denial of my right of consent as one of the governed, the denial of my right of representation as one of the taxed, the denial of my right to a trial by a jury of my peers as an offender against law, therefore, the denial of my sacred rights to life, liberty, property and—
Judge Hunt: The Court cannot allow the prisoner to go on.
Miss Anthony: But your honor will not deny me this one and only poor privilege of protest against this high-handed outrage upon my citizen's rights. May it please the Court to remember that since the day of my arrest last November, this is the first time that either myself or any person of my disfranchised class has been allowed a word of defense before judge or jury—
Judge Hunt: The prisoner must sit down—the Court cannot allow it.
Miss Anthony: All of my prosecutors, from the 8th ward corner grocery politician, who entered the complaint, to the United States Marshal, Commissioner, District Attorney, District Judge, your honor on

the bench, not one is my peer, but each and all are my political sovereigns; and had your honor submitted my case to the jury, as was clearly your duty, even then I should have had just cause of protest, for not one of those men was my peer; but, native or foreign born, white or black, rich or poor, educated or ignorant, awake or asleep, sober or drunk, each and every man of them was my political superior; hence, in no sense, my peer. Even, under such circumstances, a commoner of England, tried before a jury of Lords, would have far less cause to complain than should I, a woman, tried before a jury of men. Even my counsel, the Hon. Henry R. Selden, who has argued my cause so ably, so earnestly, so unanswerably before your honor, is my political sovereign. Precisely as no disfranchised person is entitled to sit upon a jury, and no woman is entitled to the franchise, so, none but a regularly admitted lawyer is allowed to practice in the courts, and no woman can gain admission to the bar—hence, jury, judge, counsel, must all be of the superior class.

Judge Hunt: The Court must insist—the prisoner has been tried according to the established forms of law.

Miss Anthony: Yes, your honor, but by forms of law all made by men, interpreted by men, administered by men, in favor of men, and against women; and hence, your honor's ordered verdict of guilty, against a United States citizen for the exercise of *"that citizen's right to vote,"* simply because that citizen was a woman and not a man. But, yesterday, the same man-made forms of law, declared it a crime punishable with $1,000 fine and six months' imprisonment, for you, or me, or any of us, to give a cup of cold water, a crust of bread, or a night's shelter to a panting fugitive as he was tracking his way to Canada. And every man or woman in whose veins coursed a drop of human sympathy violated that wicked law, reckless of consequences, and was justified in so doing. As then, the slaves who got their freedom must take it over, or under, or through the unjust forms of law, precisely so, now, must women, to get their right to a voice in this government, take it; and I have taken mine, and mean to take it at every possible opportunity.

Judge Hunt: The Court orders the prisoner to sit down. It will not allow another word.

Miss Anthony: When I was brought before your honor for trial, I hoped for a broad and liberal interpretation of the Constitution and its recent amendments, that should declare all United States citizens under its protecting aegis—that should declare equality of rights the national guarantee to all persons born or naturalized in the United States. But failing to get this justice—failing, even, to get a trial by a jury *not* of my peers—I ask not leniency at your hands—but rather the full rigors of the law.

(*text continued on page 12*)

The Bill of Rights:
An Expandable Document

The first ten amendments to the Constitution are often referred to as "the Bill of Rights," because they contain early and fundamental provisions for limiting the power of government and increasing the power of citizens. Bill of Rights freedoms were further enlarged by Amendments Thirteen (abolition of slavery), Fourteen (equal protection), Fifteen (Negro male suffrage), Nineteen (woman suffrage), Twenty-four (abolition of poll tax) and Twenty-six (eighteen-year-old vote), and would be expanded still more by the proposed Equal Rights Amendment. Although only the Nineteenth Amendment and the proposed ERA expressly mention women, the rights asserted in all these amendments belong to women as people and are the foundation for the continuing extension of those rights.

Amendment I: Congress shall make no law respecting an establishment of religion, or prohibiting the free exercise thereof; or abridging the freedom of speech, or of the press; or the right of the people peaceably to assemble and to petition the Government for a redress of grievances.

Amendment II: A well regulated Militia, being necessary to the security of a free State, the right of the people to keep and bear Arms, shall not be infringed.

Amendment III: No Soldier shall, in time of peace be quartered in any house, without the consent of the Owner, nor in time of war, but in a manner to be prescribed by law.

Article IV: The right of the people to be secure in their persons, houses, papers, and effects, against unreasonable searches and seizures, shall not be violated, and no Warrants shall issue, but upon probable cause, supported by Oath or affirmation, and particularly describing the place to be searched, and the persons or things to be seized.

Amendment V: No person shall be held to answer for a capital, or otherwise infamous crime, unless on a presentment or indictment of a Grand Jury, except in cases arising in the land or naval forces, or in the Militia, when in actual service in time of War or public danger; nor shall any person be subject for the same offense to be twice put in jeopardy of life or limb; nor shall be compelled in any criminal case to be a witness against himself; nor be deprived of life, liberty or property, without due process of law; nor shall private property be taken for public use, without just compensation.

Amendment VI: In all criminal prosecutions, the accused shall enjoy the right to a speedy and public trial, by an impartial jury of the State and district wherein the crime shall have been committed, which district shall have been previously ascertained by law, and to be informed of the nature and cause of the accusation; to be confronted with the witnesses against him; to have compulsory process for obtaining witnesses in his favor, and to have the Assistance of counsel for his defense.

Amendment VII: In suits at common law, where the value in controversy shall exceed twenty dollars, the right of trial by jury shall be preserved, and no fact tried by jury shall be otherwise re-examined in any Court of the United States, than according to the rules of the common law.

Amendment VIII: Excessive bail shall not be required, nor excessive fines imposed, nor cruel and unusual punishment inflicted.

Amendment IX: The enumeration in the Constitution, of certain rights, shall not be construed to deny or disparage others retained by the people.

Amendment X: The powers not delegated to the United States by the Constitution, nor prohibited by it to the States, are reserved to the States respectively, or to the people.

(Passed by Congress, September 25, 1789; ratified by the States, December 15, 1791.)

Judge Hunt: The Court must insist—(Here the prisoner sat down.)
Judge Hunt: The prisoner will stand up. (Here Miss Anthony arose again.) The sentence of the Court is that you pay a fine of one hundred dollars and the costs of the prosecution.
Miss Anthony: May it please your honor, I shall never pay a dollar of your unjust penalty. All the stock in trade I possess is a $10,000 debt, incurred by publishing my paper—The Revolution—four years ago, the sole object of which was to educate all women to do precisely as I have done, rebel against your man-made, unjust, unconstitutional forms of law, that tax, fine, imprison and hang women, while they deny them the right of representation in the government; and I shall work on with might and main to pay every dollar of that honest debt, but not a penny shall go to this unjust claim. And I shall earnestly and persistently continue to urge all women to the practical recognition of the old revolutionary maxim, that "Resistance to tyranny is obedience to God."[3]

Glued to the Pedestal

Misconceptions about women's physical and social nature, as well as the threat to male supremacy, played an important role in the strong public sentiment against women's entering political life. As one ardent opponent of women's suffrage said before Congress in 1887:

Women are essentially emotional. It is no disparagement to them they are so. It is no more insulting to say that women are emotional than to say that they are delicately constructed physically and unfitted to become soldiers or workmen under the sterner, harder pursuits of life.

What we want in this country is to avoid emotional suffrage, and what we need is to put more logic into public affairs and less feeling. There are spheres in which feeling should be paramount. There are kingdoms in which the heart should reign supreme. That kingdom belongs to woman. The realm of sentiment, the realm of love, the realm of the gentler and the holier and kindlier attributes that make the name of wife, mother, and sister next to that of God himself.

I would not, and I say it deliberately, degrade woman by giving her the right of suffrage. I mean the word in its full signification, because I believe that woman as she is to-day, the queen of the home and of hearts, is above the political collisions of this world, and should always be kept above them. . . .

It is said that the suffrage is to be given to enlarge the sphere of woman's influence. Mr. President, it would destroy her influence. It would take her down from that pedestal where she is today, influencing as a mother the minds of her offspring, influencing by her gentle and kindly caress the action of her husband toward the good and pure.[4]

Alice Duer Miller, a later suffragist and humorist, knew how to reflect such comments right back, in a form emphasizing their absurdity. One of her best pieces was inspired by Congressman Edwin Webb, who in an antisuffrage speech gallantly announced: "I am opposed to woman suffrage, but I am not opposed to woman." Miller dashed off an appropriate answer:

> O women, have you heard the news
>   Of charity and grace?
> Look, look, how joy and gratitude
>   Are beaming in my face!
> For Mr. Webb is not opposed
>   To woman in her place!
>
> O Mr. Webb, how kind you are
>   To let us live at all,
> To let us light the kitchen range
>   And tidy up the hall;
> To tolerate the female sex
>   In spite of Adam's fall.
>
> O girls, suppose that Mr. Webb
>   Should alter his decree!
> Suppose he were opposed to us—
>   Opposed to you and me.
> What would be left for us to do—
>   Except to cease to be?[5]

On another occasion, she skillfully lampooned the antisuffragists in a ditty entirely composed of favorite, but contradictory, antisuffrage clichés:

> OUR OWN TWELVE ANTI-SUFFRAGIST REASONS
> 1. Because no woman will leave her domestic duties to vote.
> 2. Because no woman who may vote will attend to her domestic duties.
> 3. Because it will make dissension between husband and wife.
> 4. Because every woman will vote as her husband tells her to.
> 5. Because bad women will corrupt politics.
> 6. Because bad politics will corrupt women.
> 7. Because women have no power of organization.
> 8. Because women will form a solid party and outvote men.
> 9. Because men and women are so different that they must stick to different duties.
> 10. Because men and women are so much alike that men, with one vote each, can represent their own views and ours too.

11. Because women cannot use force.
12. Because the militants did use force.[6]

The Nineteenth Amendment

The battle for women's suffrage was won only after more than half a century of struggle. Adopted in 1920, the Nineteenth Amendment states simply that "the right of the citizens of the United States to vote shall not be denied or abridged by the United States or by any State on account of sex." No constitutional status other than the vote was extended to women at this time, however.

In addition to the victory of suffrage, the early twentieth century brought with it renewed interest in the employment status of women. An important result of the industrial revolution following the Civil War had been the influx of workers of both sexes into the factories. Relegated to the most tedious and low-paying jobs, and often placed in very unhealthy work environments, women and children soon became the target of social concern. One response was legislation setting out special protections for women and children, among them minimum wage and maximum hours laws, and requirements for rest periods and other amenities intended to make the workplace more bearable.

Feminists played a leading role during the early part of the century in reforming women's working conditions through such organizations as the Consumers' League (1899) and the National Women's Trade Union League (1903). Both laborers and wealthy women were active in trying to improve the oppressive conditions of the factories and sweatshops, where women worked extremely long hours in stifling, unsanitary surroundings for barely subsistence pay. Indeed, because exploitation was not limited to women and children, the ultimate goal of most labor reform agitators was improved conditions for *all* workers.

Problems of Protective Legislation

However, union leaders soon indicated that they were not interested in using special legislation as a method to achieve better working conditions for their predominantly male membership. Instead, some unions began to use "protective" laws as a way of excluding women from traditionally male occupations. Rather than take the position that no one should be forced to work in unhealthy conditions, the unions often argued that women were not strong enough to withstand the strains of certain jobs—and that therefore the jobs should go to men. Thus, to the extent that special labor laws for women encouraged a public view of women as "weak" and "inferior," the original reform drive was set on its head; laws designed to "protect" women from exploitation became a barrier to their full participation in society.

An illustration of the legal consequences appears in a 1908 opinion of the United States Supreme Court upholding a special law limiting the hours of women laundry workers:

That woman's physical structure and the performance of maternal functions place her at a disadvantage in the struggle for subsistence is obvious. This is especially true when the burdens of motherhood are upon her. Even when they are not, by abundant testimony of the medical fraternity continuance for a long time on her feet at work, repeating this from day to day, tends to injurious effects upon the body, and as healthy mothers are essential to vigorous offspring, the physical well-being of woman becomes an object of public interest and care in order to preserve the strength and vigor of the race.

Still again, history discloses the fact that woman has always been dependent upon man. He established his control at the outset by superior physical strength, and this control in various forms, with diminishing intensity, has continued to the present. As [in the case of] minors, though not to the same extent, she has been looked upon in the courts as needing especial care that her rights may be preserved. Education was long denied her, and while now the doors of the school room are opened and her opportunities for acquiring knowledge are great, yet even with that and the consequent increase of capacity for business affairs it is still true that in the struggle for subsistence she is not an equal competitor with her brother. Though limitations upon personal and contractual rights may be removed by legislation, there is that in her disposition and habits of life which will operate against a full assertion of those rights. She will still be where some legislation to protect her seems necessary to secure a real equality of right. Doubtless there are individual exceptions, and there are many respects in which she has an advantage over him; but looking at it from the viewpoint of the effort to maintain an independent position in life, she is not upon an equality. Differentiated by these matters from the

other sex, she is properly placed in a class by herself, and legislation
designed for her protection may be sustained, even when like legislation is not necessary for men and could not be sustained. It is impossible to close one's eyes to the fact that she still looks to her brother
and depends upon him. Even though all restrictions on political, personal and contractual rights were taken away, and she stood, so far as
statutes are concerned, upon an absolutely equal plane with him, it
would still be true that she is so constituted that she will rest upon
and look to him for protection; that her physical structure and a
proper discharge of her maternal functions—having in view not
merely her own health, but the well-being of the race—justify legislation to protect her from the greed as well as the passion of man. . . .[7]

Disagreement over special labor laws for women eventually
caused a rift within the women's rights movement. Supporters
of the legislation sought protections for women because reform
of bad working conditions was urgently needed. Although they
would have preferred reform of conditions for both sexes, it
seemed apparent to them that such legislation would only be
enacted if it was limited to women and children. Opponents of
this special legislation warned that support for any legal distinctions based on sex was a dangerous strategy; they believed
that laws to "protect" women would be used to restrict their
opportunities in employment and in other areas.

By 1923, when the Equal Rights Amendment was first introduced into Congress, the disagreement had become so serious
that many feminists refused to lobby for adoption of the ERA.
They feared that the amendment would undermine their hard-
won labor reform gains, because such laws treated men and
women differently and might be rendered invalid under the
ERA. The debate continues to this day; today, however, the
women's movement is more united in its belief that the best
strategy is to lobby for laws which secure safe and humane
working conditions for men and women alike, while whole-
heartedly supporting passage of the ERA. This issue and others
raised by the ERA will be discussed at greater length later.

Recent Advances Toward Equality

It was not until 1971 that the United States Supreme Court
first held that a statute treating women and men differently
might violate the Constitution. In a landmark case known as

Reed v. *Reed* the Court determined that the Equal Protection Clause of the Fourteenth Amendment prevents a state legislature from passing laws which treat people unfavorably because of their sex, unless the state can offer a reasonable explanation for the difference in treatment.[8] While this conclusion appears far from revolutionary today, as the first application of the Fourteenth Amendment to women it was the greatest breakthrough for women's legal status since enactment of the Nineteenth Amendment in 1920. *Reed* v. *Reed* was the first case to place any strong constitutional restraint upon the freedom of Congress and state legislatures to discriminate on the basis of sex. The case signaled the end of the Court's historic "hands-off" attitude, and the beginning of at least minimal accountability to constitutional principles in the legal treatment of women.

In the *Reed* case, Sally Reed, an Idaho resident, sued for the right to manage the estate of her son, who had recently died. An Idaho statute, however, preferred male over female relatives as administrators of the estates of deceased persons. By automatic application of the statute, Sally Reed's husband, from whom she was separated, was appointed administrator. In appealing her case to the United States Supreme Court, Sally Reed argued that Idaho's law violated her rights under the Equal Protection Clause of the Fourteenth Amendment.

The Court framed the question as whether a difference in sex "bears a rational relationship" to the purpose which the state had in passing the law: that is, does the state have a good reason, other than prejudice or an arbitrary drawing of lines, on which to base its differential treatment of women? The state of Idaho could offer no evidence that it had actually compared the relative abilities of Mr. and Mrs. Reed to handle their son's property and personal belongings. Nor could it offer any good explanation for preferring a man over a woman, as a general matter, except that it was a convenient way to eliminate a dispute between competing relatives. The Court found that Idaho was making an arbitrary distinction not "rationally related" to the efficient management of the estate. Such an arbitrary distinction based on sex, the Court concluded, violated the Fourteenth Amendment's Equal Protection Clause.

Discrimination in the Military

Since the *Reed* decision in 1971, the Supreme Court has heard a number of other cases challenging the constitutionality of legal distinctions based on sex. As in *Reed*, the Court has at times struck down laws which treat men and women differently. For example, in 1973, in the case of *Frontiero* v. *Richardson*, the Supreme Court struck down a federal law which automatically allowed a male member of the military to claim extra housing and medical benefits if he was married, while requiring a female service member to prove that her husband was dependent on her for over half his support before she could qualify for the same benefits.[9] Citing the language of the Bradwell case as an example of traditional sexist thinking, four of the justices subscribed to the opinion that the dual benefit scheme perpetuated the outmoded view of women as dependents rather than breadwinners, and violated constitutional requirements of fairness and equality. Although the whole Court did not concur, some feminists saw that opinion as a signal that the full legal equality of women was at hand.

However, the Court has since then often refused to take a strict stand against sex-based laws. In 1975, for example, in another case involving military regulations, *Schlesinger* v. *Ballard*, the Court upheld a rule which gave women naval officers four more years during which to achieve promotion or be dismissed from the Navy than was granted to their male counterparts.[10] The Court based its holding on the "beneficial" impact of the rule on women, thereby throwing into confusion the entire issue of whether the Constitution should ever allow sex-based distinctions in the law.

Schlesinger and other cases seem to indicate the Court's approval of so-called "protective" laws for women, opening up the same issues which divided women's rights advocated early in this century. Today, however, feminists agree that the ultimate effect of every gender-based law—whether motivated by sincere beliefs about women's supposed need for special protection or by underlying biases aimed at keeping women "in their place"—is to perpetuate women's historic subordinate status. The root of the problem is that women still have not achieved express recognition of their equality with men under the Constitution itself. While racial classifications in the law are generally considered to be suspect, the Supreme Court has not consistently struck down all laws which treat men and women differently. Instead, the Court looks to whether the sex-based classification is closely related to a legitimate government purpose, thereby giving government agencies an opportunity to argue in favor of sex-based laws.

In a 1981 case, for example, all-male military registration was upheld by the Court, since women are presently excluded from combat positions and the registration is used primarily to identify possible combat personnel.[11] In the more recent case of *Roberts* v. *United States Jaycees*, however, the Court upheld the decision of the state of Minnesota that the Jaycees must admit qualified women members in order to comply with that state's anti-discrimination laws. The Court rejected the argument of the Jaycees that requiring acceptance of female members would violate the male members' constitutional rights of freedom of association and freedom of speech.[12] Six weeks later, the U.S. Jaycees voted to admit women into all of their state chapters.

The Equal Rights Amendment: Writing Women into the Constitution

As early as 1923, suffragists recognized that the Fourteenth Amendment's grant of racial equality would probably never be sufficient to end sex discrimination. In that year, an Equal Rights Amendment was first introduced into Congress. Public support for such a change was lacking for many years. Finally, in 1972, Congress passed the ERA, which declared the legal equality of women.

In order for a constitutional amendment to be adopted, however, it must be approved by at least three-fourths of the state legislatures, as well. Only thirty-five of the necessary thirty-eight states ratified the ERA by the final Congressional deadline of June 30, 1982. Since then, ERA proponents have initiated the whole amendment process again, by introducing the ERA into Congress each year in the face of a vocal opposition.

Actually, much of the opposition to the ERA stems from ignorance about women's current legal status and from misunderstanding of what the ERA would or would not do to correct present inequalities. Some people mistakenly believe that women have already achieved legal equality, or at least are satisfied with their current status. Others are personally threatened by the changes they observe in the lives of women all around them, and see opposition to the ERA as a way of putting off inevitable social change. Some women who are fulfilling traditional functions in the home see the ERA as an unwanted challenge to their way of life. Still others fear that "sex equality" in a legal sense means a "unisex" society.

Thus, one important effort of the supporters of the ERA has been to try to inform people of just what the ERA means. In simple terms, the ERA means that the sex of a person could no longer be a factor in determining that person's legal rights. In other words, the law would have to judge people on their individual needs, worth, behavior, or other relevant considerations, and not on the basis of prejudices about "man's place" and "woman's place." A state, for example, could set up requirements that a lawyer must have a certain level of legal training, competence, and moral character in order to practice law. Some women would meet these qualifications and some would not. Some men would meet these qualifications; some would not. Whatever an applicant's qualifications, the ERA would mandate that the sex of the individual is not a relevant factor. In that way, people need not be trapped by outmoded ideas about what a boy or girl, woman or man, "should" do or "should" need or "should" want, but would be supported by the law in pursuing individual goals.

Organized opponents of the ERA play on sincere fears by using half-truths and emotional arguments. One stock line of almost every ERA debate, for example, is that the ERA will require that young girls be drafted and sent to the front lines of combat. It is true that the ERA might not permit men and women to be treated differently by a military draft simply because of their sex. Individuals could be drafted and placed in appropriate work settings on the basis of such relevant factors as mental and physical

condition, family status, age, and training. Indeed, looking at individual characteristics, rather than simply at gender, is what the
ERA is all about. But ERA opponents neglect to mention that
Congress has ended the draft; and, more important, should the
draft be resumed, there is nothing to prevent Congress from
drafting women, ERA or no ERA. In fact, Congress considered the
drafting of women during World War II, but the war ended while
that decision was still pending.

The real issue, as far as women's equality is concerned, is
not who will fight where, should our military forces become
engaged in armed combat again. The issue is whether the ca-
reers and benefits available in the military should be opened up
to women who wish to pursue them. Sex equality in the military would bring to women opportunities for training, education, and other veterans' benefits which have largely been
denied to them, even in peacetime, because of severe restrictions on their voluntary enlistment and advancement in the
ranks of the armed forces.

Other anti-ERA arguments include forecasts that all women
will be forced out of the home to work, and that men and
women will have to share bathrooms, dormitory rooms, and
prison cells. As a practical matter, the ERA has little to say
about personal decisions concerning work either in or out of
the home. The need for a wage-earning spouse—whether man
or woman—to support the family is an economic, not a legal,
one. While the ERA will play a role in opening up employment
opportunities for women throughout the labor market, the
amendment itself in no way dictates how a man and woman
will make family financial decisions about the division of
work. One of the most important developments in states
which have ERA's in their state constitutions has been the
increasing recognition that the domestic contributions of a
homemaker have a value equal to that of breadwinning. In the
following chapter, we will look at a case that illustrates this
trend.

As for the famous "toilet controversy," there is no reason to
believe that equality of rights for women can be obtained only
at the expense of personal privacy or decency. Any form of

forced mixing of the sexes by the government in a way which infringes on rights of privacy would itself be subject to constitutional challenge.

Passage of the ERA is the next logical step in the move toward full legal rights for women, providing a great symbolic step forward for women's status. Without the ERA, there is no continuing mandate to the courts and the legislatures to enforce equality of rights on a daily level. If unrealistic appraisals of the present and false fears of the future do not stand in the way of the ERA, there is hope that it can bring about its real goal: to break down legal barriers between the sexes and open equal opportunity to all people under the Constitution.

TWO: Marriage and the Law

The Three Unequal Partners

MOST PEOPLE DO NOT THINK of the law as having very much to do with their family lives. The family is seen as the most private of institutions, where the wishes, desires, and values in each relationship are unique. It is not always apparent, therefore, that state laws are an ever-present force in determining the roles to be played within family relationships. The fact is that each state has its own laws which tell us when we may marry, give us a whole new set of legal rights and duties when we do marry, decide when and if we may divorce, determine to a large degree how property will be divided during and after marriage, give us rules on how to raise our children, and assign child custody if the marriage dissolves. When we decide to marry, like it or not, we are striking up a lifetime partnership not of two, as most of us imagine, but of three: ourselves, the person we marry, and the state.

In this chapter, we will be discussing traditional marriage and its history as a legal agreement. About the alternate life-

styles that have come into being in recent years, gaining increasing social acceptance, we will have little to say. That is
not because these new family arrangements are of no importance, but because for the most part our domestic relations
laws do not cover them. Marriage is defined in law as the union
of two persons of the opposite sex and, at the present time at
least, excludes the idea of marriage between two persons of the
same sex or marriage among groups of more than two individuals. To a homosexual couple, for example, this means that the
law denies them the symbolic recognition of their mutual
commitment. Similarly, a group of unrelated people living together, although they may look upon themselves as a family
and operate as an economic unit, can be legally barred from certain neighborhoods through "single family" zoning laws. It is
important to remember, however, that although the law now
refuses to recognize alternative marriages and families, this
recognition may not be far away. As these new arrangements
find greater acceptance in our society, and as their supporters
continue to pressure legislatures and courts, legal change is
likely to follow.

Similarities between Marriage and Business Contracts

The legally defined marriage with which we will concern ourselves here is in many ways like a business contract. Each party
agrees to enter a relationship in which each will give up certain
freedoms and gain certain benefits. As in most agreements between individuals, the role of the law in this marriage contract
is not obvious unless the agreement breaks down. In a contract
to buy a car, for example, no formal arm of the law is apparent
in the transaction as long as the dealer delivers the car as agreed
upon and the buyer pays the amount due on time. However,
if the dealer produces the wrong model, yet insists that the
buyer continue to make payments, a lawsuit is the probable
result. The agreement having failed, the law steps in to determine through the courts the exact duties of each party under
the contract and the remedies that can be undertaken to set the
situation straight.

In the same way, when two individuals agree to take each other as partners in marriage, there is usually no reason to resort to legal action while the marriage is healthy. The role of the law becomes clear only if something goes wrong, usually when one party seeks to end the marriage. At that point, the courts intervene to determine whether the marriage may be dissolved and to assign duties and rights to each party with regard to property, children, and ongoing support payments— matters the marriage partners probably worked out for themselves until trouble began.

Ignorance Is the Rule

This analogy should not be stretched too far, however; obviously, most marriages are based on affection as well as economics. It is perhaps for this reason that people getting married are rarely as familiar with the terms of the contract they are signing—even though it is "for life"—as are people entering even a short-term business relationship. In business contracts, both sides are usually well-acquainted with the terms of the agreement. Having drawn up the contract to fit their specific needs, they know what duties they will have to perform, what they will receive in return, and what the damages will be if they fail to live up to the obligations. Couples entering into marriage, on the other hand, may have vague notions of caring for each other "in sickness and in health," and staying together "until death do us part," but they are often totally ignorant about the financial obligations they may incur, the future ownership of their property, or the division of labor to be expected within the household.

State Laws Define the Terms

In addition, couples are frequently unaware that the questions most important to them are usually matters of law, not individual choice, and that even a formal document carefully drawn to settle some of these critical issues before marriage may be unenforceable in court. In ordinary business contracts, parties may bind themselves to any terms they please, and obtain court enforcement of their agreements, as long as they do not agree to anything actually illegal. Not so with the marriage contract. In marriage, state law itself has traditionally defined the terms of the relationship.

For example, a husband and wife might formally agree that the husband should perform a certain share of child-care duties while the wife is employed outside the home. But if the husband fails to live up to his promise, the wife would probably be unable to have the contract enforced, whether she asked the court to order him to do the work, hire a housekeeper, or pay her for doing it herself. The court would be likely to disregard the couple's formal agreement, because it runs counter to the traditional legal notion that wives are responsible for providing domestic services, while husbands are responsible for the family's financial support.

Under such circumstances, a married woman may decide to dissolve her marriage relationship, feeling that this traditional legal view does not fairly represent what she thought *her* marriage was all about. Again, however, she is subject to the law, which not only defines what a marriage should look like, but also sets out the grounds for dissolving it. While divorce in most states is far easier to obtain than it was formerly, it is still the state, not the couple, which decides when a marriage can be terminated.

Traditional Definitions of Marriage

To gain a clearer picture of the nature of the law's view of marriage, we must take a brief look at the traditional law of the family which we have inherited from English "common law" —the vast body of legal rules and doctrines, accumulated in court decisions since medieval times, which forms the basis of much of our legal tradition. While in some areas of modern law the common law has been completely replaced with new statutes and legal rules, in others it still plays a significant role. In family law, modern statutes and court decisions have changed some, but not all, of the common-law precepts. The result is a patchwork of old and new rules, with ancient and modern values coexisting and, at times, competing in our legal definition of marriage and the family.

In common law, a married woman was viewed as simply an extension of her husband. At the moment of marriage, an almost magical transformation was supposed to take place in the wife, so that in the eyes of the law her identity united with and was submerged in that of her husband. Her situation was explained in the following way in 1769 by William Blackstone, the leading writer on the English common law:

By marriage, the husband and the wife are one person in the law . . . the very being and legal existence of the woman is suspended during the marriage, or at least is incorporated into that of her husband under whose wing [and] protection she performs everything. . . .[1]

Thus the wife became a legal nonperson, a part of her husband without separate identity. Almost two hundred years later, United States Supreme Court Justice Black summed up the situation in a few well-chosen words:

This rule has worked out in reality to mean that though the husband and the wife are one, the one is the husband.[2]

Effects of the "Merger of Identities" Theory

The "merger of identities" did not take place in the realm of magical theory only. It affected the wife's life in practical terms, from marriage until the end of her life. The moment she married she lost, and her husband gained, the sole right to manage any real estate she might own. He also gained complete ownership of, not just managerial rights to, any other kind of property she brought to the marriage. A married woman could not sue or be sued; if harmed by another's actions, she had to rely on her husband to sue for her. He, not she, then became the legal owner of any damage awards won in her suit. She could not make a will, and if she worked outside the home, her wages belonged to her husband. She was required to live where he wanted to live; if she refused to do so, he could come after her and bring her back. It became her duty to perform all domestic services, including cooking, housekeeping, bearing and rearing children, and meeting her husband's sexual demands.

The husband was sole guardian of any children of the marriage, and, in case of separation, automatically obtained custody of them. In return for providing domestic services, the wife acquired the right to be clothed, fed, and sheltered by the husband.

Married Women's Property Acts

Many of the common-law restraints on married women have changed since medieval times. As a result of the political struggles of feminists, beginning in the nineteenth and early twentieth centuries, there has been a good deal of progress toward gaining legal rights for married women. Most important were the Married Women's Property Acts passed by most states in the late nineteenth century, abolishing many of the legal disabilities which had relegated married women to a position comparable to that of children and the mentally incompetent. As a result of these acts, a married woman can now own property in her own name, can sue and be sued, can run her own business, can work outside the home and claim the wages as her own, and can make a will disposing of her own property as freely as can her husband.

However, not all the incidents and by-products of the old "merger of identities" theory have disappeared. Remnants of the notion crop up frequently to remind us that married women have not yet freed themselves completely from their common-law history. For example, some states require a married woman to have the same legal residence as her husband, regardless of where she actually lives. While he can no longer physically force her to share his home, these residence laws can have more than symbolic significance in a number of situations. For one thing, a single woman attending a state-supported college in her home state has the benefit of lower tuition rates as a state resident. However, if she should marry a student from another state, she may have to pay a higher tuition: the law suddenly determines that she lives out-of-state, despite the fact that she has never left her home. She may also lose her right to vote in state and local elections, to serve on juries, or to hold office in the state where she has always lived and continues to live. Courts in recent years have heard challenges to these laws on the grounds that they violate a married woman's constitutional rights.

What's in a Name?

The loss of a woman's independent status upon marriage is perhaps most clearly illustrated in the customary changing of a woman's name to that of her husband. Names are among our most powerful personal symbols. From our earliest consciousness, our names are inextricably tied to our growing awareness of who we are, what we are like, how we differ from others, and where we fit into the society around us—in short, our identity. It is hardly surprising, then, that in a tradition defining marriage as the merging of the woman's being into that of her husband, the ceremony should be accompanied by the loss of her name and the acquisition of his.

The practice of women's adopting their husbands' names at marriage is largely a matter of custom rather than written law. In common law, any person could change his or her name simply by adopting and using the new name exclusively, as long as it was not done to deceive or defraud anyone. Based on this custom, however, many states have adopted statutes or administrative regulations which presume that a woman does, in fact, always choose to change her name at marriage. For example, in some states a woman must reregister to vote or apply for a new driver's license after marriage. Government officials, mistakenly believing that the law requires women to adopt their husbands' surnames, may refuse to allow women to maintain registrations or their formal identifications in their birth-given names. Some state provisions prevent a married woman from changing back to her birth-given name without her husband's permission; others provide that when a man changes his name, his wife's name automatically changes too. These rules of law underscore the woman's loss of self-determination at marriage, and serve to perpetuate the notion that a wife is only an appendage to her husband.

But, inevitably, the law is beginning to respond to growing pressure from women who insist upon asserting a separate identity in marriage. Typical of the new trend is a 1975 New Jersey court case, *Egner* v. *Egner,* in which a woman who was getting divorced asked the court's permission to change back to her birth-given name.[3] The lower court refused to allow this, saying that it would not be good for the young children involved to be living with a mother bearing a different last name. When the woman appealed, however, the Superior Court upset this decision, and held that a divorced woman, just like anyone else, had a right to use the name of her choice.

Obligations Imposed by Traditional Marriage Law

At the heart of the traditional definition of marriage is a basic bargain which the law assumes to take place between husband and wife—the exchange of the wife's domestic services in return for financial support from the husband. According to this "bargain" theory, a wife is obliged to perform housekeeping, childrearing, and sexual services for her husband, while he in turn is expected to provide food, clothing, and shelter for her. Whether or not it accurately describes the average marriage relationship, this breadwinner-homemaker, support-services dichotomy still pervades our social thinking and provides the fundamental principle that lies behind some of our marriage laws.

In this respect the marriage relationship may seem to resemble a contract between an employer and an employee: under the support-services "bargain," the wife offers her services in return for financial support, much as an employee works in return for her wages. However, the similarities are on the surface only. In fact, traditional legal theory relegates the female marriage partner to a uniquely dependent role, leaving her less power of self-determination than most employees can claim.

Position of the Homemaker Wife

In the first place, unlike an employee, a wife working in the house as a homemaker is not entitled to a definite wage. Instead, a wife is entitled to receive only as much as her husband chooses to give her. While the marriage lasts, the wife who has no independent income is dependent upon the financial whims of the wage-earning husband: generous husbands will provide better than miserly ones, and wealthy men better than poor men. Thus, what the wife gets is an allowance, handed out by her husband at his discretion—not wages. As legal commentator Blanche Crozier wrote in 1935, in an article in the *Boston University Law Review:*

This is precisely the situation in which property finds itself; it may be overworked and underfed, or it may be petted and fed with cream, *and that is a matter for the owner to decide.*[4]

Furthermore, as long as the homemaker wife lives with her husband, she stands little chance of getting aid from the courts if she feels her husband is not supporting her adequately. Courts have generally held that the husband-provider's discretion in such matters should not be tampered with. A modern-day example of this ancient rule is the case of Lydia McGuire, the wife of a Nebraska farmer, who complained to the state court in 1953 that although she had worked in the fields, cooked, cleaned, and washed throughout a thirty-four-year marriage, her husband would never provide for her properly. Among other things, he refused to install a bathroom or a kitchen sink in the house; to put in an adequate furnace; or to replace their outmoded wood-burning stove. He bought his wife no clothing or household goods; would not give her money to visit her grown daughters; and insisted on paying for the groceries himself, refusing to allow her to use either his money or his credit. Far from being a poor man struggling to survive, Mr. McGuire had property worth approximately $200,000.

Court Refuses to Interfere

While noting that Mr. McGuire had a "reputation for more than ordinary frugality," the Nebraska court decided that Lydia McGuire had no case, and dismissed her petition for additional support. The court held that although Mr. McGuire had a legal

(text continued on page 34)

A Giant Milestone:
Married Women's Property Acts

From the middle of the nineteenth century until the early part of the twentieth century, Married Women's Property Acts were passed in most states, to do away with many of the legal disabilities of married women with regard to possession, management and transfer of real estate and other assets. Women began to gain control over their own earnings and property, as well as rights to contract, sue, and conduct business in their own names.

Laws passed by the New York state legislature between 1848 and 1892 are illustrative of the types of new provisions adopted across the country during this era. Excerpts from the New York legislative Acts, given on these pages, afford a glimpse into half a century of step-by-step legal reform.

An Act for the more effectual protection of the property of married women *(passed April 7, 1848)*: . . . The real and personal property, and the rents issues and profits thereof of any female now married shall not be subject to the disposal of her husband; but shall be her sole and separate property as if she were a single female except so far as the same may be liable for the debts of her husband heretofore contracted.

It shall be lawful for any married female to receive, by gift, grant devise or bequest, from any person other than her husband and hold to her sole and separate use, as if she were a single female, real and personal property, and the rents, issues and profits thereof, and the same shall not be subject to the disposal of her husband, nor be liable for his debts.

An Act to amend the foregoing act *(passed April 11, 1849)*: . . . Any married female may . . . convey and devise real and personal property, and any interest on estate therein, and the rents, issues and profits thereof in the same manner and with like effect as if she were unmarried. . . .

An Act concerning the rights and liabilities of husband and wife *(passed March 20, 1860)*: The property, both real and personal, which any married woman now owns, as her sole and separate property; that which comes to her by descent, devise, bequest, gift or grant; that which she acquires by her trade, business, labor or services, carried on or performed on her sole or separate account; that which a woman married in this state owns at the time of her marriage, and the rents, issues and proceeds of all such property, shall, notwithstanding her marriage, be and remain her sole and separate property, and may be used, collected and invested by her in her own name, and shall not be subject to the interference or control of her husband, or liable for his debts, except such debts as may have been contracted for the support of herself or her children, by her as his agent.

Any married woman may, while married, sue and be sued in all matters having relation to her property, which may be her sole and separate property, or which may hereafter come to her by descent, devise, bequest, or the gift of any person except her husband, in the same manner as if she were sole. And any married woman may bring and maintain an action in her own name, for damages against any person or body corporate, for any injury to her person or character, the same as if she were sole; and the money received upon the settlement of any such action, or recovered upon a judgment, shall be her sole and separate property.

An Act to authorize and empower a husband to convey directly to his wife and a wife directly to her husband *(passed June 6, 1887)*: Any transfer or conveyance of real estate hereafter made by a married man directly to his wife, and every transfer or conveyance of real estate hereafter made directly by a married woman to her husband, shall not be invalid because such transfer or conveyance was made directly from one to the other without the intervention of a third person.

obligation to support his wife, the court would not tell him
how to go about doing it:

The living standards of a family are a matter of concern to the household, and not for the courts to determine, even though the husband's
attitude toward his wife, according to his wealth and circumstances,
leaves little to be said in his behalf. As long as the home is maintained
and the parties are living as husband and wife it may be said that the
husband is legally supporting his wife and the purpose of the marriage
relation is being carried out.[5]

Only if Mrs. McGuire decided to separate from her husband
could she rely on the courts to help her secure adequate support for herself.

Mrs. Hardy's Allowance

The support-services model of marriage differs from an employment contract in other ways, too. Unlike an employee, a
homemaker wife may not necessarily do whatever she likes
with money she receives as support—in other words, it does
not actually belong to her. And, as we saw before, even if a
husband-provider voluntarily agrees to pay the wife-home-
maker a definite amount in return for her work, a court may
not hold him to it. A case in point is that of Mr. and Mrs.
Hardy, who during their marriage made an agreement concerning housework. Up until that time, Mr. Hardy had been giving
his wife $125 per week for household expenses, part of which
had been used to pay a maid. With her husband's approval, Mrs.
Hardy decided to let the maid go and assume the cooking and
cleaning responsibilities herself, in exchange for the money she
could save from the household allowance. During the several
years that this arrangement lasted, Mrs. Hardy did all the
housework and invested the money she saved in stocks. At the
time of their divorce in 1964, her husband found out about her
investments and sued, saying the stocks were bought with his
money and thus belonged to him.

The court agreed. According to the judge, the money Mrs.
Hardy had received for running the household over the years
was not hers to use as she pleased, as the housemaid's wages
had been; in fact, the couple's agreement was worth nothing in

the court's eyes, since the wife was obligated under the marriage "bargain" to perform domestic services anyway. Rather than outright pay, the money she received was treated by the court as a kind of expense account, to be used only for certain limited purposes:

The court recognizes that such household allowances generally comprehend expenditures by the wife for personal needs such as clothes, entertainment and transportation. Such expenses are within the obligation of the husband to support and maintain his wife. Acquiescence in these expenditures does not indicate an acquiescence in the use of such funds for the wife's sole account. To hold otherwise would be to invite disruptive influences in the home.[6]

It seems that the court would not have objected had Mrs. Hardy saved the money to buy a dishwasher, an automobile, or even a fur coat, all of which are "normal" desires for a middle-class housewife. It was the completely independent use of the money for her own economic security that the court found unacceptable.

Mrs. Glover's Misbehavior

As the *Hardy* case indicates, a woman straying from the behavior expected of a housewife is in danger of receiving a slap in the face from the court, a slap which can have severe economic consequences. The further she strays from her role, the more punitive the court may be. In the 1970 New York case of *Glover* v. *Glover*, for example, a divorced woman was denied support from her husband, who had a substantial law practice. According to the court, Mrs. Glover "drove [her husband] to distraction" by her "grievous and loathsome" misconduct:

The court finds that petitioner [Mrs. Glover], who was obsessed with the desire to be in business for herself despite the respondent's repeated requests to her to give up her business ventures and take care of the home, and despite the fact that he had already yielded to petitioner and given her no less than $2000, for her business ventures which he opposed, went behind respondent's back and approached several of his legal clients and friends to loan her money or co-sign loans for her. . . .

On several occasions respondent [Mr. Glover] was compelled to entertain clients alone at his home and cook the dinner for them, since petitioner, who was aware of the social engagements, came home several hours late, and on two occasions . . . came home at about 12 midnight.

. . .one of respondent's witnesses testified that petitioner's home was a mess. . . .[7]

In sum, the court felt, Mrs. Glover was "a most attractive, articulate, and youthful-looking woman, apparently in her forties, but fiery, volatile, ruthless, self-centered, cunning, and uncompromising"—and completely undeserving of a support order. Little attention was given to whether or not she needed support in order to survive.

Experiments in Redefining Marriage

Nowadays, increasing numbers of couples are rejecting sex-stereotyped concepts of marriage, such as the support-services model. Instead, they favor more equal arrangements, which recognize the unique abilities and potential for growth of each partner. To express their discontent with traditional marriage definitions, many people create individual marriage contracts, in which they outline their plans for shaping their own marriages. Tailored to the individual beliefs and expectations of the parties, these contracts can be valuable tools for devising creative, practical alternatives to customary wife and husband roles. For example, many couples have been able to find ways to share the provider and domestic functions; in this way, they make sure to recognize the value of the homemaker role, whether it is performed by the husband, the wife, or a combination of the two. Morally binding, if not legally so, these contracts are an important part of the gradual redefinition of marriage taking place today.

Some Early Dissenters

Although finding greater acceptance today, the idea of alternative marriage agreements is far from new. In 1855, feminist Lucy Stone and her husband, Henry B. Blackwell, wrote and signed the following document:

PROTEST. While acknowledging our mutual affection by publicly assuming the relationship of husband and wife, yet in justice to ourselves and a great principle, we deem it a duty to declare that this act on our part implies no sanction of, nor promise of voluntary obedience to such of the present laws of marriage, as refuse to recognize the wife as an independent, rational being, while they confer upon the husband an injurious and unnatural superiority, investing him with legal powers which no honorable man would exercise, and which no man should possess. We protest especially against the laws which give to the husband:

1. The custody of the wife's person.
2. The exclusive control and guardianship of their children.
3. The sole ownership of her personal, and use of her real estate, unless previously settled upon her, or placed in the hands of trustees, as in the case of minors, lunatics, and idiots.
4. The absolute right to the product of her industry.
5. Also against laws which give to the widower so much larger and more permanent an interest in the property of his deceased wife, than they give to the widow in that of the deceased husband.
6. Finally, against the whole system by which "the legal existence of the wife is suspended during marriage," so that in most States, she neither has a legal part in the choice of her residence, nor can she make a will, nor sue or be sued in her own name, nor inherit property.

We believe that personal independence and equal human rights can never be forfeited, except for crime; that marriage should be an equal and permanent partnership, and so recognized by law; that until it is so recognized, married partners should provide against the radical injustice of present laws, by every means in their power.

We believe that where domestic difficulties arise, no appeal should be made to legal tribunals under existing laws, but that all difficulties should be submitted to the equitable adjustment of arbitrators mutually chosen.

Thus reverencing law, we enter our protest against rules and customs which are unworthy of the name, since they violate justice, the essence of law.

(Signed)
Henry B. Blackwell,
Lucy Stone.[8]

A particularly eloquent dissent, even earlier than the Stone-Blackwell declaration, was the "Marriage Document" of feminist Mary Jane Robinson and her husband, Robert Dale Owen, before their marriage in 1832. In this statement, Owen vehemently refused to accept the rights of almost total domination which the laws of the nineteenth century still awarded to him as a husband:

> . . . Of the unjust rights which in virtue of this ceremony an iniquitous law tacitly gives me over the person and property of another, I can not legally, but I can morally divest myself. And I hereby distinctly and emphatically declare that I consider myself, and earnestly desire to be considered by others, as utterly divested, now and during the rest of my life, of any such rights, the barbarous relics of a feudal, despotic system, soon destined, in the onward course of improvement, to be wholly swept away; and the existence of which is a tacit insult to the good sense and good feeling of this comparatively civilized age.— *Robert Dale Owen*
> I concur in this sentiment.—*Mary Jane Robinson*[9]

New Marriage Contracts

Many of today's marriage contracts go into greater practical detail than the statement fashioned by Robert Dale Owen and Mary Jane Robinson. They cover a wide range of topics, depending on which issues a couple sees as important. Some contracts deal solely with the property rights of the couple; some describe how household work should be divided; some set out grounds for dissolving the marriage. There are contracts providing intricate mechanisms for arbitrating disputes, and even setting up systems of fines and penalties for violation of the agreement.

Probably the most important subject addressed by modern marriage contracts is the allocation of what has long been considered "women's work"—cooking, cleaning, and raising children. As we have seen, the traditional support-services model of marriage requires the wife alone to perform these tasks, with little in the way of financial security to reward her. The following excerpt, from a model contract between parties given the fictitious names of Donald and Ina, shows how a couple might come to terms with this "bargain theory" in the light of their individual goals and needs:

> It is the parties' present intention that Ina continue to work, health permitting, until such time as she may become pregnant. The parties

have no exact intentions concerning the employment of Ina after the birth of any child or children, although Ina has expressed the feeling that simply caring for children would not be sufficiently stimulating to her. Donald's inclination at the present time is that he would prefer for Ina to discontinue any full-time employment if she had a child, but he would not insist upon it.

Both parties agree that any subsequent employment of Ina after the birth of a child should be such that it would permit her to spend reasonable periods of time with the child and that it should not entail any evening or weekend hours.[10]

From this statement, it appears that both Donald and Ina view the primary childrearing responsibility as hers. Therefore, although they allow for a good deal of flexibility in the arrangements Ina might ultimately make, she will almost certainly face a limitation of her earning power when children are born. To make sure that Ina will be economically compensated for her child-care work, the contract includes carefully detailed financial arrangements, requiring that a joint checking account be set up, with contributions to it proportionate to each party's income; providing for the joint ownership of property; and establishing the way funds will be divided in case of divorce. By this device, the contract formally recognizes that Ina's household work will have an economic value of its own, and at the same time guarantees her a measure of economic independence.

Will the Courts Go Along?

As we have seen earlier in this chapter, individual marriage contracts may not always be enforceable in court; if one party doesn't live up to the agreement, a court may refuse to remedy the grievance because the judge believes that certain provisions in the contract vary too widely from the law's traditional conception of marriage. However, the parts of Donald and Ina's contract concerning division of property would almost certainly be upheld, since agreements concerning division of property, such as Donald and Ina's, are routinely enforced by courts —and have been for centuries. On the other hand, an arrangement obliging Donald to pay Ina wages for her housework, or to perform certain domestic tasks himself, would meet a less

certain fate. So far, so few such marriage contracts have actually been brought to court that it is impossible to predict the
judicial reaction.

The Community Property System

There are indications, however, that the legal system is moving
toward a recognition of marriage as a partnership of equals rather
than a relationship where one party is dominant and the other
dependent. Early in the nineteenth century, some southern and
western territories began adopting a "community property" system of marriage. In force today in eight western states, community property laws hold that almost all money and property acquired by one spouse during a marriage automatically belongs to
the "community" of the marriage—that is, to both partners
equally. While this has not always meant that the wife was entitled to equal *control*—in some states the husband had the sole
right to manage the property—the concept of equal ownership is
an important protection for homemaker spouses who are dependent on the wage-earner for economic survival.

By contrast, in all other states, which have what is called a
"separate property" system, the wage-earner has traditionally
been the sole owner of her/his earnings. While in the event of
death a surviving wife (or husband) usually had an automatic
right to a portion of the deceased spouse's estate, neither during
the marriage nor at divorce did a wife have any absolute right to
even part of her husband's property, despite having contributed
to the marriage through her work as a homemaker.

The Uniform
Marriage and Divorce Act

Even in "separate property" states, however, recent legislation shows a tendency on the part of lawmakers to move away
from the unequal support-services model toward a partnership
model of marriage. In an attempt to bring order to the chaos of
existing state marriage and divorce laws, an independent commission has drafted the "Uniform Marriage and Divorce Act,"
which is offered to state legislatures as a model which each

state is free to adopt or reject. Already adopted at least in part by most states, the UMDA may provide a glimpse into the future of family law, if present trends continue.

The UMDA treats division of property at divorce in much the same way as is done in community property states. Money and property acquired by either spouse during the marriage are considered "marital property," which at the time of divorce is to be divided between the spouses. (During the marriage, however, each spouse may own his or her property separately.) At the time of divorce, the judge is required to divide up the marital property according to the needs and financial abilities of each spouse, as well as the contributions each spouse made to the marriage. Significantly, the UMDA states that homemaking contributions should be considered, as well as economic ones, an approach now adopted by thirty-six states. The UMDA also shifts emphasis in property divison away from blame and toward financial needs—a significant departure from former law, which so harshly punished the independent-minded Mrs. Glover.

A New View of Alimony

Alimony—the ongoing payment of basic support money by one divorced spouse to the other—is also awarded under the UMDA on the basis of financial needs and abilities, not blame. As everyone knows, alimony situations are fraught with problems. Wage-earners (usually husbands) resent the continuing burden of providing for a former spouse and frequently fail to pay; the receiver of alimony, who because of child-care responsibilities and a lifetime out of the job market is often desperately in need of the money, is frustrated by her demeaning dependence on an unreliable allowance. For these reasons, the UMDA favors providing for the needs of divorced people by property settlement, rather than through alimony payments. Ideally, this arrangement allows each spouse to make a fresh start financially, free of future economic ties to the other. In practice, however, alimony is still necessary in some cases, because divorcing couples rarely have enough property to provide adequately for each spouse. Where alimony is awarded, the UMDA urges judges to encourage training and reentry into the job market, so that the support payments need not go on indefinitely.

UMDA urges judges to encourage training and reentry into the job market, so that the support payments need not go on indefinitely.

"No-fault" Divorce

The UMDA covers other aspects of marriage and divorce law as well. For example, under the UMDA, divorce is available on the grounds that the marriage has "irretrievably broken down." This idea of "no-fault" divorce, which has by now been adopted in one form or another by most states, means that a person seeking a divorce need no longer prove to a court that her or his spouse was guilty of certain misconduct, such as adultery or physical cruelty. Under the UMDA, where the marriage has obviously failed, a divorce may be obtained regardless of who was at fault.

Child Custody: A Step Forward

A third important innovation of the UMDA is its attempt to set forth uniform guidelines to determine which parent ought to have custody of the children. In the past, judges received little guidance from state law when faced with this difficult decision, beyond a simple statement that the "best interests of the child" should be considered. Consequently, custody decisions were often based on a judge's personal beliefs or prejudices, with widely varying results. For women this usually meant automatic custody, except for those mothers whose lifestyles were seen as unconventional. Now, written guidelines are used in most states, including the wishes of the child, the child's current attachment to parents, siblings, and other significant community members, and the physical and emotional health of each parent. The overall standard is the best interest of the child.

Perhaps the most significant trend in custody laws in the 1980s has been the increasing preference for joint custody. Under joint custody both parents retain legal authority over the child's care, with physical custody being shared between them. Proponents of joint custody maintain that divorce should not necessarily result in the separation of children from one of their parents.

Positive Effects of State ERAs

A final word in this chapter should be given to the effect of the proposed Equal Rights Amendment on the law of marriage and divorce, and to the effects already felt in states where equal rights amendments have been added to state constitutions. Opponents often claim that the ERA could result in financial harm to dependent homemaker women, taking away their right to alimony or forcing them to support children on their own. However, in states with equal rights amendments, experience shows that the ERA has had exactly the opposite effect, and that it is actually able to strengthen a homemaker's rights to marital property.

A case in point is the 1975 Pennsylvania decision entitled *DiFlorido* v. *DiFlorido,* where a divorced husband tried to get possession from his former wife of all the family's household goods, such as furniture and appliances, based on the fact that as the wage-earner he had paid for them.[11] At the time, Pennsylvania law was on his side: under traditional common-law doctrines, a judge had to award all such property to a husband unless the wife could prove she had bought it with her own money. The Pennsylvania Supreme Court, however, ruled that Mrs. DiFlorido's twelve years of work as a homemaker were as valuable to the marriage as her husband's work as breadwinner; therefore, even though she had not actually paid for the household goods, she was entitled to half of them. The old rule, according to the Court, violated the state Equal Rights Amendment because it ignored the substantial work customarily performed by women. Under this reasoning, a homemaker's right to alimony, child support, and various kinds of property would be strongly supported by the proposed national Equal Rights Amendment.

The Equal Rights Amendment, the Uniform Marriage and Divorce Act, and individual marriage contracts are all signposts that lead in a common direction. Although they cannot tell us precisely what our future legal definition of marriage will be, they do indicate that the old support-services model is gradually giving way to a legal view of marriage as a partnership of equals.

THREE: Women and Employment

Injustice in the Marketplace

IN 1973, STELLA PULASKI was feeling pretty fed up with the kind of work she was doing. She had held a lot of clerical jobs and had done some electrical assembly work. She was now working in the library of a daily newspaper, and she hated it. She had gone to school to learn offset printing, and wanted to practice her new craft, but she couldn't get a job in printing.

"Everybody wanted to know if I could type, but I knew I couldn't support myself and my kid on a clerk's job. Then I heard that the Telephone Company was hiring women for traditionally male jobs because of a lawsuit against them, so I applied for a 'craft job,' like installer or repair person. When I said I wanted to be an installer, the man told me it wasn't an entry-level job. I knew that wasn't true, because I had read that they were supposed to take women for craft jobs as a high priority, so I wasn't buying what he said, and I told him so. I took some tests in math and language and some in mechanical aptitude and spatial relations, and a physical examination.

"I had to keep calling for about two weeks, but finally the man asked if I wanted to be a splicer's helper. I didn't know what it was, but he said it was working outside, so it sounded just fine to me."

The Trials and the Satisfactions

"My job was mostly helping set up the manhole. The splicer goes down the hole, and I stand on top and hand him tools and keep people away from the opening. The men were very nervous the first week. I think they didn't know how to act. They asked me a lot of questions about why I wanted a job like this.

"As time went by, they got used to me and had more confidence in me. A lot of my job is to protect the splicer, and I think at first they were afraid that if a problem came up, I wouldn't be able to handle it. For instance, a splicer could pass out in a manhole. That never happened, though.

"Probably the hardest thing for me to take is the amount of ridicule I get from men on the street. I get comments like 'Why aren't you home cooking dinner?' or 'Is this what women's lib is all about?' One guy offered to take me home and show me how to cook spaghetti. I try to ignore them, but it really gets to me. Any time I try to reply, they only get more hostile. I've never gotten negative remarks from women, though. In fact, one time, a little old woman about seventy came up and said she had worked on the railroad during the war and she thought it was wonderful that I was doing this kind of work. Things like that make all the negative comments easier to take.

"Another great thing about the job is that I'm making more money than I've ever thought I would make. I think, though, that even if the money weren't so good, I would still do it, because I get a lot of satisfaction out of my work."

"Ma" Bell's History of Discrimination

If Stella had applied for a "craft job" with the phone company any time before 1973, she probably would have been turned down outright. The problem would not have been Stella's alone. Because the Bell System is the largest private employer of women in the nation, Bell's discriminatory policies have affected the employment scene for women in serious ways for a good many years.

The Bell System, until recently headed by American Telephone and Telegraph, has a long history of both race and sex segregation. Initially, the telephone industry employed only white males. In 1878, one local phone company, concerned that male operators were sometimes "noisy, boisterous, and rude," experimented by hiring the first female operator, Emma Nutt. She was a success, and the idea spread. Since women would work for one-third of what men were paid, women were soon used extensively in operator and clerical jobs. Before long, those jobs became defined strictly as "female" jobs, just as they had once been exclusively "male" jobs.

Until the 1970s, the major departments within the Bell System were almost totally segregated by sex, with "craft jobs"—meaning repair and installation—reserved for men, and "traffic jobs"—operators and clerks—left for women. The "female" jobs paid much lower wages and consisted mostly of routine, dull, regimented work, with rules governing every aspect of behavior on the job, including dress and conversation at the switchboard. Opportunities for promotion were virtually non-existent for traffic jobs, while craft jobs offered men the chance to advance to managerial rank. In fact, men from other departments were often promoted to higher levels of management within the Traffic Department, while women rarely if ever reached supervisory rank in any section of the system. Occasionally, a local phone company might define a particular craft job as "female," but the women who filled these slots were always paid less for their work than the men who performed exactly the same duties in other localities throughout the country.

In addition to phone company policies which discriminated outright against women, there were also many rules which seemed neutral, but had the effect of discriminating against women workers. For example, one phone company had a rule that all persons in craft jobs must be at least 5'6" tall. The rule was applied equally to men and women. However, anyone looking around at the average heights of women and men can see that such a rule would have the effect of keeping many more women than men out of craft jobs.

Finally, women were often at a disadvantage in the Bell System because of various penalties levied against pregnant workers. For example, many local phone companies forced pregnant women to leave their jobs, sometimes many months before the expected birth. No regard was given to whether the woman wanted or needed to keep working, or even to whether her doctor felt she was physically fit. On the other hand, on those days when a pregnant woman was physically unable to work, she was usually denied the right to any form of sick pay.

A Woman's Place:
Low- or No-paying Jobs

Bell's policies were typical of attitudes toward women in the job market. Throughout American history, women have been prohibited from entering many types of employment, and have occupied the lowest-paying ranks of others. Although people have been fond of saying that a woman's place is in the home, this has not been true: since the industrial revolution, a woman's place has also been in the factories and mills, where she and her children have earned the lowest wages, amid dangerous, unhealthy conditions; a woman's place has also been working on the farm alongside her husband, at times doing heavy manual labor. A woman's place has not, however, been in the professions, in the higher-paying industrial jobs, or even in the unions. With the exception of the radical Industrial Workers of the World, the American labor movement of the nineteenth and early twentieth centuries systematically excluded women from its leadership—and often even from its membership.

The law itself was often simply a reflection of the social values that allowed this discriminatory scheme to exist. When women turned to the courts in the latter half of the nineteenth century to seek the right to follow certain professions, such as the right to practice law, they found no support from an all-male legal system. Indeed, the courts continued to enforce the unequal treatment of women in the workplace for the next hundred years.

The Question of "Protection"

One battle which raged for many years was the question of whether women needed special laws regulating their working conditions. As noted in the chapter on constitutional law, a "protective" law for women was upheld by the United States Supreme Court in 1908, based on the view of women as weaker creatures than men.[1] A similar law affecting male bakers in New York had been struck down three years earlier, on the grounds that it interfered with their right to contract for as many hours of work as they wanted.[2]

Of course, many of these so-called "protective" laws for women were passed out of a sincere concern for the shocking conditions under which people worked during the early part of this century: unsafe factories, extremely long hours, and pitifully small wages. Many feminists, as we noted in Section One, supported the struggle for protective laws for women. Others, however, soon became disenchanted with labor laws that applied to women only. Why should women be limited in their work opportunities in this way? Weren't all people, not just the female sex, deserving of decent, humane working conditions? The true nature of the protective laws became even more obvious later in this century, as women who had held good jobs during the world wars found themselves being displaced by returning soldiers. The excuse for laying off these women was often that it was for their own "protection." But the reality was that many "protective" laws, such as those limiting the weight women were allowed to lift, or the number of hours they might work, mainly functioned to protect certain work opportunities for males.

A classic example of how women became the victims of "protection" occurred when men reentered the domestic labor market in large numbers following the end of World War II. During wartime, women had successfully filled many jobs usually restricted to men, ranging from heavy-duty industrial work to bartending. In 1945, the male-controlled bartenders' union in Michigan managed to secure the enactment of a special state law restricting a woman from bartending unless her

husband or father owned the bar. While this law was upheld by
the United States Supreme Court in 1948 under the guise of
"protecting" women, no evidence was offered to show that
women either wanted or needed such "protection."[3] Indeed, it
was widely recognized that the real interest behind this law
was in protecting bartending jobs for male union members.

Antidiscrimination Laws and Remedies

It was not until 1963 that the first federal law was passed reflecting the principle of sex equality in the workplace: the
Equal Pay Act forbade employers to pay different salaries to
men and women who do equal work.[4] This landmark law was
quickly followed by Title VII of the Civil Rights Act of 1964,
which in broad, comprehensive terms, forbade discrimination
on the basis of race, sex, or religion in any of the terms or conditions of employment.[5] The principle underlying Title VII is
that people should be judged on their individual merits, not on
generalizations about sex or race or religion.

Ironically, Title VII, a product of the Civil Rights movement
of the 1960s, was designed with race discrimination in mind,
not sex discrimination. In the last days of the heated debate
which preceded passage of the Act, opponents of the bill engi-
neered an amendment to forbid sex, as well as race, discrimination, apparently feeling that such a provision was so ludicrous
as to ensure the defeat of the entire bill. The bill passed anyway, however, and in this back-door fashion one of this country's most important pieces of legislation for women was enacted.

AT&T: An Unprecedented Victory

The Bell case offers an example of antidiscrimination legislation operating at its best. Stella Pulaski, along with thousands of other women and members of minority groups, owes
her job directly to a case against American Telephone and Telegraph, based on Title VII and the Equal Pay Act. After a wide-
scale investigation of unfair practices, the Equal Employment
Opportunity Commission, the federal agency which enforces
Title VII, met with AT&T to work out what eventually devel-

oped into the largest and most comprehensive civil rights settlement ever agreed to in this country. All aspects of AT&T policies—pay scales, departmental structures, hiring, firing, and recruitment—were covered in the agreement. Local phone companies were given time limits for placing minorities and women in all levels of the company, and a special government committee was set up to monitor compliance with the affirmative action order. The total damage award to minority and female employees, to compensate them for wages lost through past discrimination in hiring and promotions, amounted to thirty-eight million dollars.

Federal courts have had many other occasions for applying Title VII to charges of unfair discrimination. These court decisions illustrate the way the principles of Title VII are applied. For example, while Title VII broadly prohibits employment practices expressly based on sex, the law does provide for one exception: an employer can defend a sex-based hiring policy if it can be shown that the sex of the applicant is a "bona fide occupational qualification," or BFOQ, as it is commonly called.

When Is a BFOQ Not a BFOQ?

Naturally, many employers have tried to raise a BFOQ defense when charged with unfair hiring policies based on sex. For example, AT&T claimed that being female was a BFOQ for the job of operator, because men do not have the helpful, nurturing personality characteristics thought to be desirable in an operator. Similar claims have been raised by the airline industry to defend the policy of limiting flight attendant jobs to women. During a Title VII suit brought against Pan American Airlines by a man seeking to become a flight steward, the company argued that it was justified in accepting only female applicants, because women attendants were "better, in the sense that they were superior in such nonmechanical aspects of the job as providing reassurance to anxious passengers, giving courteous personalized service, and, in general, making flights as pleasurable as possible within the limitations imposed by

(text continued on page 54)

Class Action Suits:
Taking the Big Ones to Court

The 1970s marked an era of large-scale class action lawsuits, charging employers with sex discrimination in employment practices. These practices often went hand-in-hand with discrimination against racial and ethnic minorities. The excerpts below are taken from charges brought in the autumn of 1974 by the New York State Division of Human Rights against a major publishing company.

Upon information and belief respondent Publishing Company maintains an employment policy, which has resulted in creating and perpetuating certain categories of jobs that are filled predominantly by women and certain other categories of jobs which are filled predominantly by men.

Women comprise 94% of the lowest three levels of editorial positions (editorial assistant, assistant editor, and associate editor) while men comprise 76% of the highest three levels of editorial positions (senior editor, managing editor, and executive editor).

Sales positions, in particular those of college traveler, commission salesman, salesman, and sales representative, are almost exclusively filled by men. Repondent's Trade Department alone has 26 men in such sales positions but no women.

College-educated women, including some with graduate degrees in English, who want to enter the publishing field, are employed by respondent Publishing Company as secretaries and editorial assistants.

College-educated men with comparable backgrounds, who want to enter the publishing field, are employed by respondent Publishing Company in sales, accounting, and finance-related positions which offer greater opportunities for mobility, promotion, and salary advancement.

Women hired as editorial assistants are led to believe that they will receive training and experience in editorial skills and functions together with opportunities for advancement within the company. In fact it is often difficult to differentiate the assigned tasks of the editorial assistants from those of secretaries, typists, and receptionists.

Women employees of respondent Publishing Company perform work comparable to that done by male employees who hold higher positions and receive greater pay.

Women employees, in particular editorial assistants, assistant editors, and associate editors, are bypassed for promotions for which their experience and background qualifies them.

Respondent Publishing Company hires women almost exclusively in low-paying job categories and expects them to compete with each other for the few token promotions to higher level positions granted to women after years of service to male superiors.

Respondent Publishing Company's job titles are ill-defined and inconsistent from division to division and department to department, which enables respondent to hire women in titles that do not correspond to their actual jobs.

Of some 370 professional, managerial and technical employees at respondent Publishing Company, blacks, hispanics and orientals comprise only 18, or less than 5%.

Respondent Publishing Company maintains a college recruiting program but does not include efforts to recruit minority students for the above categories of jobs.

Respondent Publishing Company has engaged and is engaged in a position and practice of discrimination in employment against blacks, hispanics and orientals on the basis of race or national origin.

aircraft operations." The court looked behind Pan Am's argument to consider whether it is true that *no* man could fill these specialized job functions, since Title VII requires that each individual be looked at on his or her own merits. In addition, the court noted that while a male steward "is perhaps not as soothing on a flight as a female stewardess," this was really beside the point in terms of an airline's basic business purpose, which is to transport people efficiently and safely to their destination. The court also rejected the argument that airline customers prefer female attendants, concluding that none of these rationales was sufficient to establish a true BFOQ.[6]

The BFOQ defense has also been rejected in situations in which an employer refuses to hire any women because of the strenuousness of the job. The courts have uniformly concluded that excluding all women from jobs involving, for example, heavy weightlifting, based on blanket assumptions about women's physical capacities, is exactly the kind of unfair practice which Title VII was designed to correct. The solution is not to rule out all women, but to test the ability of each applicant to perform a given job. Using an unbiased test, some women would undoubtedly pass, and some men would fail.

Indeed, the only situations in which the Equal Employment Opportunity Commission has recognized the validity of a sex-linked job description are in the limited areas of acting and modeling, where sexual characteristics are intrinsic to performance, or in jobs where specific biological functions are required, such as wet nurse or sperm donor. A recent decision of the United States Supreme Court has widened this exception somewhat, holding that women may in some cases be excluded from prison guard jobs in maximum security units for men, because the extreme danger of sexual attack could lessen their effectiveness in maintaining order.[7]

When Is a "Neutral Rule" Not Neutral?

Presenting another difficulty for Title VII enforcement are employer policies which, though neutral on their face, have an unfair impact on women. Policies such as the former rule in some phone companies that all job applicants be at least 5'6" tall are typical of this kind of "neutral rule," under which many women lose out. These cases can raise complicated issues, because two competing interests are at stake, both of which represent legitimate concerns. On the one hand, employers must have some freedom to set realistic criteria in looking for the people best qualified to do a job. On the other hand, women and minorities must not be excluded en masse from certain jobs because of rigid hiring rules which have little to do with the skills needed to do the job. A high school diploma, for example, may be an important requirement for some jobs, such as secretarial work, where a fairly high level of reading and writing skills is essential. But what about a rule requiring a high school diploma for certain maintenance jobs? This kind of work does not necessarily require advanced reading skills or formal skills in writing. A rule requiring a high school diploma would only screen out large numbers of minority applicants in the many areas of the country where blacks and other members of minority groups have historically been deprived of equal educational opportunities.

The "Business Necessity" Test

In order to determine which "neutral" employment policies unjustifiably burden women or minorities, the courts use a device known as the "business necessity" test. Unless an employer can show that a hiring policy that works against women or minorities actually measures an ability that is related to the job in question, the practice will be struck down. Courts have used this standard to invalidate employment practices, regardless of whether the employer intended to discriminate, since the effect of discrimination is as damaging to the victim as bad intent would be.

However, applying the "business necessity" doctrine can present problems of its own. Particularly in management-level jobs, employers often insist that "how a person fits in" can be as important to performing the job as skills which can be measured by a test. One of the most difficult challenges in the development of equal employment law is to devise ways to prevent employers from using the need for subjective judgment as a screen for sex discrimination, while still allowing the latitude necessary for employers to select well-qualified people.

In 1984, the Supreme Court rejected a large law firm's argument that its partners needed latitude to make subjective judgments about whether a particular young lawyer associated with the firm should be made a full partner. Title VII, the Court said, prohibits professional partnerships from denying partnership status to women by applying subjective double standards as barriers to women's successful promotion.[8] A contrary decision could have been a blow to women's advancement in fields such as law, accounting, investment banking, real estate, advertising, and other professions in which partnerships are the common business structure and the old boys' network remains strong.

Affirmative Action Policy

The doctrines just discussed deal with the problem of deciding when discrimination against an individual person has occurred. An equally important, and even more difficult, question concerns what we are willing to do to remedy civil rights violations practiced over many years against whole groups. It is one thing to award money or a job to the particular individual who has proved her case. It is quite another to devise ways for whole groups of people to overcome the barriers which have historically excluded them from equal access to the job market. The latter is the underlying purpose of Title VII and other civil rights legislation of the 1960s, and to achieve it a policy of "affirmative action" has been adopted by many employers.

In the context of Title VII, affirmative action means that, in addition to ordering a defendant to give back pay or promotions to specific victims of discrimination, courts may require the employer to make special efforts to increase hiring opportunities for members of disadvantaged groups. Or, as in the case of AT&T, the employer may, during the course of negotiations with the EEOC, agree to take such steps. The employer may be required to provide special training for minority groups and women, to mount an intensive recruitment drive, or to try to increase the company's percentage of minority or female employees according to a timetable. This kind of affirmative action is well established as a means of remedying Title VII violations and compensating a class of people for past discrimination. In addition, many other affirmative action plans are undertaken by public and private employers who wish to improve job opportunities on their own, not waiting until they are formally charged with discrimination. For example, the United States government requires private employers to institute affirmative action programs if they desire to contract for work with the government.

Some Thorny Problems

The reason for the controversy surrounding affirmative action is obvious: where there are not enough jobs to go around, giving them to one class of persons means taking them away from another. For instance, if an affirmative action order requires raising the seniority levels of black workers, some white workers may be passed over. Special efforts to recruit first-rate female candidates for jobs may result in bypassing good male candidates who formerly could have counted on getting the job. Some people feel that this is unfair; that now we have "reverse discrimination," which is no better than the old kind. The Supreme Court has had to grapple with this issue on several occasions. In 1978, in *University of California* v. *Bakke*, the Court ruled that a white student, who was more academically qualified than some minority applicants who were accepted into the medical school under an affirmative action quota, had a right to be admitted to the school also. The Court did not, however, bar schools from considering race altogether in their efforts to admit more minority students.[9] A year later, the Court ruled in favor of Kaiser Aluminum Company, which had a special employee training program for which it voluntarily reserved one-half of the slots for minority employees. A white male employee who was denied entrance into the program was found not to have been unfairly discriminated against by the company.[10] More recently, however, in a 1984 decision regarding firefighters in Memphis, the Court dealt a blow to many existing affirmative action plans. Black firefighters in that city had previously settled a discrimination case by getting the city to implement an affirmative minority hiring plan. When the city later had to lay off many of its firefighters, the Court refused to protect the black workers against a "last hired, first fired" rule, thus effectively wiping out the impact of all recent minority hiring efforts.[11]

How the dilemmas caused by affirmative action should be resolved is a difficult social issue. Many opponents of affirmative action fail to give due weight to the fact that the women and minorities who benefit from such efforts have not previously had access to equal opportunity in American life. Without affirmative steps to make up for lost time, many members of these groups will never be able to compete on an equal basis for desirable jobs. How society chooses to respond to this complex problem will have a crucial impact on the progress of women and minorities in the job market.

Progress Has Been Slow

The need for continuing action to equalize employment opportunities for women is underscored by recent statistics. Although women now make up close to one-half of the total work force, they are still largely sex-segregated into the lowest paying jobs, many of which are being phased out by newly-automated information technology. As late as 1981, the median income of white women was $5,519 and of black women was $4,903 per year, compared with $14,296 for white males and $8,501 for black males. In that year, approximately 65 percent of all working women earned less than $8,000, compared with approximately 30 percent of their male counterparts.[12] An ever-increasing number of people in this country living in poverty are women or members of female-headed households. It is figures like these which have led social commentators to note that there has been a "feminization of poverty" during the 1980s.

Many people believe that greater equality in the workplace will only be achieved by attacking the disparity in women's earning power at its root—the undervaluing of work traditionally performed by women. Not until job categories dominated by women are paid at a rate comparable to job categories dominated by men, in accordance with the actual skill, effort, responsibility, and working conditions required for each type of job, will women begin to achieve true economic equality in the marketplace. Efforts to achieve "pay equity" for women move one step beyond "equal pay for equal work" to a demand for equal pay for work which women perform which is not the same as a man's work, but which should carry the same value in the society. The struggle for pay equity is currently being waged by women civil service workers in a number of states, primarily through court suits.[13] As of 1984, at least one state, Minnesota, was actively implementing wage parity for its female-dominated civil service categories on a voluntary basis, and it is expected that several states which are studying similar plans will follow in that state's footsteps.

Special Issues Related to Insurance

Employment-related insurance benefits have been another area for sex discrimination litigation in recent years. In 1976, working women were handed a setback when the Supreme Court refused to find illegal sex discrimination in General Electric's policy of excluding pregnancy-related medical disabilities from its employee insurance plan.[14] Shortly thereafter, Title VII was amended by Congress to state expressly that differential treatment of pregnant workers in the terms and conditions of employment, including insurance benefits, is unlawful sex discrimination. Since that time, the Supreme Court has outlawed traditional employer practices of requiring women employees either to pay more of their wages into employee retirement funds or to receive lower monthly benefits after retirement.[15] These unequal payment schemes were premised on the fact that women live longer than men, on the average, and thus receive retirement funds for a longer period. Treating a particular woman differently, based on some average fact about her sex, is not acceptable, said the Court. In 1984, Congress also passed the Retirement Equity Act. This new law provides for more equitable treatment of women in pension plans generally. Among other features, it allows a one-year maternity/paternity leave without jeopardizing future pension rights and gives women the right to the pensions of husbands who die before retirement age.

What The Future Holds

Civil rights legislation has been a useful, if at times limited, tool in the struggle for equal employment opportunities for women. Nothing short of a basic change in social attitudes will cause women to be admitted to the employment world on a completely equal basis with men. Such change comes slowly. As Stella Pulaski says:

"The phone company still discourages women from getting these new jobs. There are only a few women working as splicers' helpers in the city, and no women splicers. I've had an application in to become a splicer for over two years. I had a friend who applied for an installer's job and they put her in such a bad neighborhood she couldn't take it and had to go back inside.

"The brochures they put out tell you how many openings were filled with white, black, Spanish-speaking men or women, but they don't seem accurate. Last year the report said nobody was promoted to splicer, but I know three men who were promoted.

"I really like my job, though. I don't know why everybody makes such a big deal about it. I think I do it really well. Why shouldn't I?"*

* Stella Pulaski is an imaginary name for a real person whom the authors interviewed before writing this chapter. Because she was afraid of losing her job, she asked us not to use her real name.

FOUR: Women and Their Bodies

The Right to Control

A SONG THAT BECAME POPULAR among women in the early seventies started, "Our faces belong to our bodies; our bodies belong to ourselves." Something so simple and obvious hardly needs stating, one might think; yet, for some reason, these words evoked powerful emotions, and this chant could be heard over and over at demonstrations and at music and theater programs. Why such response to so basic a concept?

Women do not have control over their own bodies. For women who have sexual intercourse with men, no method of birth control is totally safe and effective. Abortion is not freely accessible. In many states, sexual behavior between members of the same sex is against the law. All women, from babies to grandmothers, are exposed to the crime of rape.

With the support of the women's movement behind them, more and more women are coming forward with accounts of physical violence experienced within their family structures. Reported incidences of incest, wife battering, and marital rape continue to grow during the 1980s, with recent studies indicating at least one out of ten women having experienced some form of sexual abuse as a child and an even higher percentage experiencing significant physical or psychological abuse within marital relationships. Strong networks have formed to provide supportive services to women who have been victims of rape, incest, and battering, and almost every state has enacted legislation during the past decade to strengthen the legal protections and remedies available to these victims.

Since sexuality and a woman's right to control her own body are such highly charged issues in our society, women who challenge traditional social and legal attitudes in these areas often encounter strong opposition. What is it about a woman's desire to control her body that creates such furor?

Rape

The most violent form of men's seizure of women's bodies is, of course, rape. Yet in most ancient cultures the law treated rape primarily as a crime against property—a man's property—and linked the act to the theft of a virgin's bride-price, which would be substantially reduced if a daughter became "damaged goods" due to having been raped. In medieval England, rape came to be used as a method of acquiring through marriage the lands of propertied virgins. In her book *Against Our Will: Men, Women, and Rape,* Susan Brownmiller described this process:

Gothic literature has made heiress-stealing a subject of great romance, replete with midnight assignations, loyal maidservants, and a great thundering of horses' hooves, but in actuality it was predicated on the desire for land, not love. If a captured virgin managed to escape before her forced marriage, or if an errant knave had merely taken her on the spot, she could attempt to seek redress in the court of her lord's manor. Trial for capital crime in those days was by physical ordeal, and grueling tests by water and hot irons were probably employed to arrive at the "truth."

. . . During the tenth-century rule of King Athelstan, if a man were to throw a virgin to the ground against her will, "he forfeits the King's grace; if he shamelessly disrobes her and places himself upon her, he incurs the loss of all his possessions; and if he lies with her, he incurs the loss of his life and members." Vengeance did not stop at death, for

... "even his horse shall to his ignomy be put to shame upon its scrotum and tail, which shall be cut off as close as possible to the buttocks." A similar fate awaited the rapist's dog, and if he happened to own a hawk, "Let it lose its beak, its claws and its tail."

After his animals were cropped and his own human life was taken, a rapist's land and money were supposed to be given to the ravished virgin. But one manner of redemption was possible. As a benevolent way of saving him from terrible death, a raped virgin might be permitted by King and Church to accept her ravisher in marriage. Since consolidation of property was uppermost in the minds of men, we may assume that a violated virgin was encouraged or *not* encouraged toward matrimony depending on which arrangement of the land was most beneficial, or least inconvenient, to the domain of Church and King.[1]

Obviously, modern concepts of the crime of rape center more on the notion of the intrusion on the person of the victim without her consent than on a tactic for building feudal holdings. Nevertheless, the view of woman-as-property persists, as in the many state laws which still hold that a husband cannot rape his wife, since with marriage he acquires an automatic right to her sexual services. The year 1984 brought the first rape conviction, in a Florida case, of a man who sexually assaulted and kidnapped his wife while the couple were legally married and residing together. Since this case, other state courts and legislatures are reconsidering the outmoded and discriminatory standard that a woman's consent is not required for sexual contact within marriage.

The Two Faces of Eve: A Cherished Stereotype

Today, social and legal attitudes toward rape are extremely contradictory, reflecting the conflicts society is experiencing as women begin to assert themselves as independent human beings. Two images, the rape victim as whore and the rape victim as innocent virgin, exist side by side in our legal treatment of rape, each representing an unrealistic, sex-based stereotype which only serves to hinder effective law enforcement. The result is that, while the incidence of reported rape continues to rise, the conviction rate for rape remains one of the lowest of all types of crime.

The Victim As Criminal

The first image is reflected in the fact that a woman who has been raped is often made to feel like the criminal rather than the victim. The entire legal process seems to assume that she is lying, that she must have initiated the contact, or at the very least invited attack through provocative clothing or behavior. For example, until recently most state rape laws included special requirements of proof, based on the premise that the woman's statement was untrustworthy. One version of this kind of law requires "corroborating evidence"—evidence in addition to the victim's statement—that shows forcible sexual intercourse has in fact taken place: cuts and bruises on the woman's body, for example, or a witness to the incident. Such corroboration requirements almost ensure that a rapist who forces a woman's submission at gunpoint, leaving her unscarred, will not be convicted. The suspicious attitudes about women underlying the corroboration requirements are well illustrated in the following remarks from a 1970 article in a law journal:

The incidence of false accusations and the potential for unjust convictions are perhaps greatest with sexual offenses. Women often falsely accuse men of sexual attacks to extort money, to force marriage, to satisfy a childish desire for notoriety, or to attain personal revenge. Their motives include hatred, a sense of shame after consenting to illicit intercourse, especially when pregnancy results, and delusion. In cases of delusion, the woman may describe the attack in remarkably convincing detail, for she herself believes her story but fails to appreciate the significance and consequences of the accusation. "Most women," according to a prominent psychiatrist, "entertain more or less consciously at one time or another fleeting fantasies or fears that they are being or will be attacked by a man. Of course, the normal woman who has such a fantasy does not confuse it with reality, but it is . . . easy for . . . neurotic individuals to translate their fantasies into actual beliefs and memory falsifications. . . ." These neurotic individuals can often deceive the most astute judges and jurors into believing that the imagined attack actually occurred.[2]

Another manifestation of this kind of thinking is the common legal practice of focusing rape trials on the woman's prior sexual conduct, as if to say that a woman who has had any prior sexual activity is necessarily of such loose moral character that she either permitted this particular act, did not discourage it, or, at any rate, deserved it. Defense attorneys routinely use this device to turn the tables on the prosecuting witness, bringing up for public view the woman's entire past and present private life, and converting the court proceeding into an ordeal where the victim, rather than the defendant, seems to be the one on trial. Then, as if that were not enough, many state laws permit the judge to wind up the trial by instructing the jury to be particularly suspicious of the testimony of an alleged rape victim. In no other type of criminal case is a judge allowed to prejudice a jury in this fashion.

Steps toward Reform

Fortunately, concerted efforts by women in the past several years have resulted in substantial progress toward the normalization of rape laws and the elimination of special, obviously biased requirements. In many states, corroboration requirements have been repealed, and the practice of attacking the victim's reputation strictly limited. Moreover, public pressure on police and district attorneys has resulted in the establishment, in some localities, of special rape squads and training for police officers to increase their understanding of rape as a serious crime; these programs have been highly successful in changing police attitudes which used to lead many officers to treat rape victims as if they were lying, questioning them skeptically about their clothing and suggesting that they provoked the attack. While these changes may result in more rape convictions, it is important to realize that they place no special burdens on persons accused of rape, who of course still benefit from the constitutional protections afforded all defendants in the criminal justice system. The reform of rape laws simply means that they must conform to the rest of the criminal law, thereby eliminating some of the disadvantages which placed the rape victim in a unique category.

(text continued on page 68)

The Crime of Rape:
Myths, Facts, and Consequences

Our laws on the violent crime of rape operate in such a way as to protect the rapist rather than the victim. Rape laws are supported by widespread myths that exert a strong influence upon those who make the laws and upon society as a whole. It was not until the early 1970s that women began to assemble the facts that contradict the myths. While police and court practices are slowly responding to pressure from organized feminists, the myths persist, making progress difficult.

The continued belief in these myths has real consequences, not the least of them in legal practices. Such consequences appear clearly when police and courts focus on the dress, behavior, and prior conduct of the victim, rather than on the attacker; in state laws holding that rape of a wife by a husband is not rape; in the "corroborating evidence" requirement which makes convictions unobtainable if the victim has escaped bodily injury.

Myth: Most rapes are committed by strangers, against women out alone at night.
Facts: Between ⅓ and ⅔ of all rapes occur in the victim's home or in some other private residence. Rapes occur at all hours. About 50% of all rapists are known, at least slightly, by their victims. The rapist is often a relative, a friend, or some other trusted acquaintance.

Myth: Rapists are identifiable by their physical appearance, actions, or words; conversely, anyone who looks "normal" or respectable is not a rapist.
Facts: The vast majority of rapists do not look or act demented; psychotic rapists are the exception, not the rule.

Myth: Women precipitate rape; they ask for it.
Facts: Police files indicate that no more than 4% of rape victims were clothed in a manner the police classified as "provocative." Being flirtatious or showing interest in sex, further, is not asking for *rape,* which is an attack in which the victim's life is controlled by the attacker. No one asks for such an assault. A hitchiker is asking for a ride, not for a violent attack.

Myth: Rape is an impulsive act of sexual gratification; the rapist is helpless to control it.

Facts: Between 60% and 75% of rapes are planned in advance; another 10% are partially planned. Ninety per cent of rapes involving multiple offenders are planned. The primary motives revealed by most convicted rapists are aggression, dominance, and hatred, not sexual desire. Most rapists have readily available sexual outlets, and over half are married at the time of the rape.

Myth: "Good girls" don't get raped; it is only "bad women" who get raped.

Facts: Rapists attack women of all races, ages, social backgrounds, and moral persuasions—housewives, hitchikers, sophisticates, and prudes.

Myth: Women enjoy rape; they should "relax and enjoy it."

Facts: Rape is not sexual pleasure for the victim. It is violence, pain, degradation, and a situation in which a woman fears for her life. Even women who have "rape fantasies" imagine surrendering to the passion of someone to whom they are already attracted. Such fantasies have nothing in common with the brutality, humiliation, and terror of rape. A true rape fantasy is a nightmare.

Myth: There is no such thing as rape. A woman can resist her attacker if she wants to.

Facts: The first concern of a rape victim is to survive, to live through the attack. No one but the victim can assess at the time of the attack what her danger is, what she is capable of doing, and what methods might succeed. Insisting that women struggle to the death rather than submit to rape is actually a way of telling women that their lives are less valuable than their sexual integrity.

Adapted from a worksheet, "Myths and their Consequences," prepared by the Minnesota National Organization for Women (NOW) State Task Force on Rape, April 1976.

At the other end of the scale is the second image of the rape victim, that of the innocent virgin. Until 1977, some states actually inflicted the death penalty on convicted rapists, an extreme response rooted in chivalric notions that a woman's purity and chastity had been irretrievably despoiled and must be avenged. Like its counterpart, this belief serves mainly to cloud the issue by focusing on the character of the victim, rather than on the fact that forcible sexual intercourse is always a crime. In addition, in those states which inflicted the death penalty for rape, "jury nullification"—the refusal of juries to convict because of their belief that the punishment is too harsh—resulted in almost no rape convictions being obtained. The exceptions occurred in the southern states, where accusations of black-on-white rape have long functioned as a means of oppressing black males.*

In 1977, the United States Supreme Court restored some balance by holding that the death penalty, when inflicted for rape, constituted cruel and unusual punishment in violation of the Eighth Amendment to the Constitution.[3] The Court found that although, "short of homicide, [rape] is the ultimate violation of self," by contemporary standards of justice the death penalty is grossly excessive where a life is not taken. Along with the legislative reforms currently taking place, this decision represents an important step toward the demystification of rape and the encouragement of a sane, realistic policy of law enforcement to combat the crime.

The Right to Choose Parenthood

The unwillingness of society to regard a woman's body as her own is equally evident in the area of a woman's reproductive

---

* While the issue is too complex for lengthy discussion here, it is important to bear in mind the connections between the oppression of black people and white women in attitudes about interracial rape. Particularly in the South, the chivalric notions about the purity of white women have been used as a weapon against black men through rape laws. According to Rep. Julian Bond, "Since 1930, 455 men have been executed for rape; 405 were black men, and all but two were executed in the South" (Southern Poverty Law Center mailing, 1976). As for the situation of black women, the law in the North and South has often ignored the rape of black women, by white men or black, and has generally been applied to discriminate. There has never been an execution of a white man for the rape of a black woman.

process. Becoming a mother means a total life change. It calls upon a woman to make an irrevocable, lifelong commitment in terms of emotional involvement, financial burdens, and loss of freedom. Yet, historically, the last person to have any control over whether and when pregnancy occurred was the woman. If married, she did not have the right to deny sex to her husband. Until recently, artificial methods of birth control were hopelessly unreliable. And as soon as more effective methods to prevent pregnancy were developed, society and law makers fought vehemently to deny women access to this means of controlling their bodies and their lives.

"Woman's Biological Servitude to Man"

Margaret Sanger, the greatest pioneer working for women's right to birth control, felt firsthand the force of legal and societal opposition to her goals. As a nurse in New York City's poverty-stricken ghettos in the first decades of this century, she daily witnessed the plight of women who could do nothing to prevent constant pregnancies—and who frequently died from attempted home abortions. While as a trained nurse she was aware of birth control methods which could have prevented much of this misery, New York's laws—similar to laws in every state of the country—made it a crime for her to teach her patients about contraception or give them any birth control devices. The injustice of this dilemma inspired her to devote her entire life's work to changing these laws, educating the world about the need for birth control, and establishing birth control clinics—all with the aim, in her words, of ending "woman's biological servitude to man."

Sanger brought a new perspective to the subject of contraception. A strong feminist, she believed that the right to vote, the right to own property, and the right to enter professions— issues considered highly crucial by most feminists of her day— were all of secondary importance compared to the need of women to be able to control their own bodies; other rights seemed to her to be of little use, as long as anticontraception laws placed control over a woman's reproductive system in the hands of male legislatures and a male medical profession.

Moreover, Sanger believed that because men wished to retain control over the numbers of children born, they would not readily yield to humanitarian arguments in favor of birth control. Her belief was reinforced by comments such as those a German physician made to her when she visited his hospital shortly after World War I. Sanger had asked the physician why it was that in Germany abortion was legal, inexpensive, and freely available to women, while contraceptive techniques were almost unknown. Why not prevent pregnancies rather than resort to the much more drastic alternative of abortion? The doctor replied: "We will never give over the control of our numbers to the women themselves. . . . With abortions it is in our hands; we make the decisions, and they must come to us."[4]

The Intrepid Margaret Sanger

Sanger's confrontations with established anticontraception forces were inevitable and frequent. The first such encounter came when her publication *Woman Rebel* was banned from the mails, and Sanger was subjected to federal prosecution on the grounds that promotion of birth control was "obscene." While these charges were ultimately dropped, arrests for distributing information on birth control remained a common fact of life throughout her career. In 1916, Sanger tested the validity of a New York anticontraception law by establishing a clinic in Brooklyn, where she and her supporters advised hundreds of women about available methods of birth control. The clinic was raided and closed nine days after its opening, and Sanger was arrested. The court did not heed Sanger's arguments that the New York law was unjust and unconstitutional, and sentenced her to thirty days in prison.

Throughout her long struggle, Margaret Sanger and her followers had a profound effect upon public opinion. Slowly her cause gained acceptance and favorable coverage in the press until a large segment of popular opinion strongly supported the idea of birth control. However, the fight was a long one, and Margaret Sanger did not live to see the end of it. While some states did liberalize their birth control laws, others kept strict anticontraceptive statutes on the books. It was not until 1965 that the United States Supreme Court took the first small step toward recognition of reproductive freedom as a right fundamental to our society, by holding that a state could not constitutionally ban the sale of contraceptives to married people.[5] That decision was followed in 1972 by another, which announced that similar laws aimed at unmarried persons were also unconstitutional.[6] The state's argument that it had a right to discourage "illicit" sexual relations was not convincing to the Court, which indicated that the punishment of forced pregnancy for such conduct seemed a bit extreme.

A Less-than-perfect Victory

As the first legal statements of a right to contraception, these cases were a vital step in the struggle of women for control over their bodies. However, it is interesting to note that the justices of the Supreme Court did not really see the issue in those terms. Instead, the Court based its decisions primarily on the theory that anti–birth control laws were unconstitutional because they attempted to regulate what went on in the bedroom, intruding on the intimacy of personal relationships, and, said the Court, interfering with a constitutionally-based "zone of privacy." Thus, these crucial decisions turned on the concept of a right of sexual privacy for the couple—an important and far-reaching concept, to be sure—but did not state categorically that a woman has a basic right to determine for herself whether and when she will become pregnant. In fact, the Court issued no strong articulation of a woman's right to control over her own reproductive processes until it handed down the abortion decisions of 1973.

The Shift in Public Opinion

To a great degree, the Supreme Court's pronouncements on birth control coincided with a shift in public opinion toward increased acceptance of contraception. By 1965, laws outlawing contraception were considered by many to be outmoded, almost quaint. The subject of abortion, on the other hand, still evokes extreme emotional responses and continues to be the focus of dramatic and bitter political struggle. Opponents of abortion usually express the belief that to terminate a pregnancy is to take a life, and urge laws prohibiting abortion to enforce their belief that the procedure is morally wrong. The other, "pro-choice" side of the argument emphasizes the right of a woman to choose whether to bear children, viewing the decision to end or to continue a pregnancy as a private, individual, ethical decision.

Woman-killers:
The Antiabortion Laws

Surprisingly enough, laws restricting or forbidding abortion are relatively new to this country. Until the middle of the nineteenth century, most states had no abortion statutes at all. A woman could easily obtain a legal abortion during the early part of her pregnancy, before the fetus had "quickened," or moved for the first time. As for later abortions, while there was some disagreement about their legal status, they were generally either unrestricted or not considered a very serious crime. Only in the middle to late nineteenth century did the states begin to enact more stringent antiabortion statutes, motivated at least in part by reformists' concerns about the then dangerous and primitive techniques which often caused death or serious injury to women. Ironically, at the same time that states were outlawing abortion with increasing severity, rapid advances in medical knowledge were converting early abortion into a relatively safe medical procedure, involving less risk to a woman's health than actual childbirth. Antiabortion laws therefore had the unforeseen result of causing thousands of women to die from illegal back-street abortions in unsanitary surroundings, when their deaths could easily have been avoided through use of properly supervised medical procedures. The laws, in effect, made safe pregnancy termination available only to the wealthy, and did little to stop the flourishing black market to which poor and middle-income women turned in their desperation.

A Woman's Constitutional Right to Decide

Gradually, in the late 1960s and early 1970s, as women exerted pressure for more freedom of choice, some states began to rewrite their laws. In a few states, such as New York, abortion became quite easily obtainable. But the most dramatic change came about in 1973, when, in the famous cases of *Roe* v. *Wade*[7] and *Doe* v. *Bolton*,[8] the Supreme Court at last took the position that the Constitution of the United States protected a woman's right to decide whether to terminate an early pregnancy (still with the proviso, however, that her doctor must concur). According to these decisions, the critical time for determining whether abortion may be prohibited is the point when the fetus becomes "viable," or able to live outside of the mother's uterus. Before viability, the same "right of privacy" to which the Court alluded in the birth control cases protects the woman's right to choose whether or not to bear a child, and society may not force her to carry to term an unwanted pregnancy. Specifically, the Court held that a state may not outlaw or restrict abortion during the first twelve weeks of pregnancy, the period when abortion is safest and the fetus is not considered viable. After twelve weeks, state laws may regulate abortion to ensure that the more complicated procedures required at that stage of pregnancy are safely executed. However, when the fetus clearly becomes viable, a time usually thought to be the twenty-fourth to twenty-eighth week of pregnancy, state laws may prohibit abortion altogether, except where childbirth will jeopardize the life of the mother.

Rights Remain in Peril

Unlike the birth control decisions, the *Roe* and *Doe* opinions did not lay to rest the controversy over society's proper response to abortion. Organized and vocal groups are still working tenaciously to counter the effects of the Court's decisions, using a variety of strategies ranging from enactment of state laws designed to limit the availability of abortion to proposals for a constitutional amendment to overrule the Supreme Court's decision.

Particularly remarkable during the 1980s has been the sharp rise in physical violence against abortion clinics through firebombings, trespassing, vandalism, and daily harassment of clinic staff and patients. Women who have worked hard to ensure the right of all women to reproductive freedom are now finding that the struggle must continue, if that right is not to be taken away bit by bit.

One common legal tactic for limiting the right to abortion has been a variety of state laws regarding consent provisions. Some of these have included detailed consent forms and waiting periods for the women themselves; others have attempted to require spousal or parental consent for a woman or teenager who wishes to terminate a pregnancy. The Supreme Court has found that such consent provisions violate the woman's right to privacy in her decision-making process, with the possible exception of a case where a parent or judge may need to intervene on behalf of a very young or otherwise immature teenager.[9]

Another common type of legal restriction has focused on the availability of public funding for abortions. The U.S. Congress and a number of states have systematically passed legislation since 1973 to eliminate federal and state funds from certain categories of abortion services. Under the Reagan Administration, for example, funds for abortions have been withdrawn from health plans that cover federal employees and military personnel. The most severe impact has been felt by low-income women and teens, as many of these funding restrictions have been aimed at federal and state subsidies for low-income health care, such as Medicaid. Low-income women who cannot afford to pay for their own medical care have in effect been forced by such laws to continue unwanted pregnancies. It was widely believed when these laws were first passed that they would be found unconstitutional. Not only do they severely interfere with a poor woman's freedom of choice, supposedly protected in the 1973 court decisions of *Roe* and *Doe*, but they also discriminated unfairly between the rights of poor women and those of more affluent women who can purchase their own medical care.

Low-Income Women: "Let Them Eat Cake"

To the surprise of many, the Supreme Court has refused to overthrow such funding restrictions on poor women's access to abortions. In a set of cases heard in 1977, the Court found that a state could not prohibit abortions for low-income recipients of medical assistance programs, but, on the other hand, states are not obligated to pay the costs either. In a blistering dissenting opinion, Justice Harry Blackmun wrote:

> . . . for the individual woman concerned, indigent and financially helpless, . . . the result is punitive and tragic. Implicit in the Court's holdings is the condescension that she may go elsewhere for her abortion. I find that disingenuous and alarming, almost reminiscent of "Let them eat cake."[10]

Another grave threat to women's right to choose has come in the form of proposed constitutional amendments. The goal of these amendments is to overthrow the Supreme Court's 1973 rulings and outlaw abortion throughout the country. Such an amendment could be adopted in one of two ways. It could be adopted by two-thirds of Congress and then ratified by three-fourths of all the states. The alternative is for two-thirds of the states to petition Congress for a constitutional convention, with any resulting amendments needing three-fourths ratification again by the state legislatures. Efforts to adopt such amendments have thus far been thwarted at the first stages of each alternative process. The success of an anti-choice amendment to the Constitution would leave women and the courts without recourse, except through the extremely difficult process of repealing the new amendment itself.

Some Unanswered Questions

In each of the areas discussed in this chapter, law reform came about only after long and intense political struggle. Moreover, continued work is necessary to prevent the erosion of rights that women have won already. Even so, issues of rape, domestic vio-

lence, birth control, and abortion only represent small parts of
the overall question of the right to control one's body. For example, hostility toward homosexuality is still prevalent in the law.
It is true that there are some local statutes designed to prevent
discrimination against homosexuals in employment and in
housing, but these are rare. Courts continue to uphold statutes
prohibiting homosexual acts between consenting adults and zoning ordinances excluding all but traditional family groups. Many
women whose lesbianism has been made an issue in child custody cases have lost custody of their children.

Another important question for women arises in the context
of sexual harassment of female employees by male employers,
where the woman's job security is frequently dependent on her
willingness to grant sexual favors. Until recently, a woman
confronted with the unwanted sexual attentions of a male
supervisor—and his subsequent retaliation if she failed to comply—had no legal remedy for her plight. Courts saw such incidents as personal interactions between men and women, rather
than as a species of gender-based discrimination against
women employees as a group. Recent surveys and speakouts by
women workers, however, have begun to bring about wider
awareness that sexual harassment on the job creates an atmosphere of fear and retaliation for working women, and severely
handicaps their job opportunities and security. Some progress
can now be seen in legal responses to these realities. In a 1976
case, for example, the court held that an employer who is aware
of and tolerates sexual harassment in the workplace is guilty of
sex discrimination. [11]

Prostitution laws present yet another set of unanswered
questions about who actually controls a woman's body. These
laws punish a female for using her body for financial gain, yet
often fail to penalize the male who purchases her services. Why
should this disparity exist? Should prostitution even be illegal?
Many people argue that the criminalization of prostitution is
just another way in which society denies women the right to
use their bodies as they choose. Proposed solutions vary. Some
people advocate "decriminalization," which would eliminate,
or reduce the severity of, the criminal offense of prostitution.

Others would substitute some form of civil regulation, similar to the present system in Nevada, where prostitution is legal but subject to strict licensing requirements.

One final area of concern for women's bodily integrity is the treatment of women in the media, especially in pornography. Women are frequently portrayed in sexually demeaning ways and in ways which promote sexual violence against women. The most recent attempt by feminists to halt the onslaught of pornographic images in our society has been through local legislation which defines pornography as a form of sex discrimination and thereby allows severe legal restrictions against its production, sale, or distribution. Because the content of pornographic writings and pictures can arguably be seen as protected by constitutional rights of free speech, such laws create tension between two competing constitutional rights: freedom from sex discrimination and freedom of speech. The first of these legislative prohibitions against pornography, passed in Indianapolis, was recently overturned by a federal judge as a violation of free speech rights.[12]

All of these questions bear on the as yet unrealized right of women to be free to control their own bodies, and all are sure to be raised continually in both the judicial and legislative arenas, as women exert continuing pressure on the legal process to recognize and protect the right to bodily privacy and integrity. It will be a long, hard fight before women can truly say with the song, "Our bodies belong to ourselves."

Conclusion

IN THIS BOOK WE HAVE DISCUSSED some of the major areas in which the struggles for women's legal rights have been and continue to be waged. As we have seen, women's legal rights are changing rapidly both in the home and on the employment front. In addition, women have obtained considerable legal rights to control their reproductive processes, although these rights remain under challenge—particularly for poor women, whose access to abortion, as a practical reality, is left to the will of each state.

New Opportunities and Old Tensions

As women make increasing strides into traditionally male sectors of the labor market, new questions are beginning to arise concerning the meaning of "sex equality." Certainly, equality for women means equal opportunity with men to pursue a chosen path in life, free from discrimination based on stereotypes and generalizations about "woman's place." As more obvious barriers to equal opportunity in employment and other public pursuits fall, the underlying tensions between these new opportunities and women's traditional homemaking roles—tensions which have always been part of the movement for women's legal rights—are resurfacing in new forms.

To date, the women's movement has focused primarily on the right of women *not* to play roles traditionally reserved for them. One effect of equal employment law, for example, is that women need *not* be tied to the home if they choose, instead, to enter the job market. The right *not* to bear children, if that is a woman's desire, now enjoys certain constitutional protections. Even the laws of marriage are beginning to respond to demands for changes in the traditional rights and responsibilities of females and males.

Motherhood: The Economic Penalties

Much less has been accomplished to ensure that women can begin to integrate both traditional and nontraditional roles, without being unfairly burdened by their choices. For example, truly equal opportunity for women must take into account that only women bear children, and that in our culture women are likely to shoulder primary responsibility for raising children for some time to come. Thus, the movement for equal rights will have to fight not only for the right *not* to bear children, but for the equally compelling right to bear and raise children without discrimination, as well. While society pays lip service to the social value of motherhood, the fact remains that the choice of motherhood is more often penalized than supported by our social structures. The Supreme Court's 1976 denial of disability benefits to pregnant workers (in *General Electric* v. *Gilbert*) is a disturbing reminder that when hard dollars are at issue, bearing a child may be considered of less value than recovering from a broken leg.

Breakthrough Areas: Credit and Housing

The law is slowly beginning to address some of the ways in which women who raise families have been handicapped in the economic arena. Two examples are the Equal Credit Opportunity Act (ECOA) and the National Fair Housing Act, both passed in 1974. Like other antidiscrimination statutes, such as Title VII of the Equal Employment Opportunity Act, these laws directly prohibit sex discrimination in particular areas of daily life—credit and housing—in which women have always been treated less favorably than men. But these laws have begun to be interpreted to extend beyond the simple situation in which a woman who applies for a credit card or a mortgage receives less favorable treatment than a man in the same circumstances with a similar income and credit history.

To take just one example, banks and department stores frequently refuse to count child support or alimony payments as "real" income in judging whether an individual can afford a particular type or level of credit. As a result, many people who rely on child support or alimony as a steady source of income may be unable to get loans or buy consumer items on credit simply because this type of income is considered unreliable. Of course, the people most likely to be receiving child support or alimony at this stage in our history are women. Thus, even though a male applicant might also have trouble if he were relying on child support or alimony to establish credit, the fact of the matter is that women form the vast majority of the victims of this unfair policy. Under the ECOA, a blanket refusal to consider these forms of income is now prohibited as sex discriminatory. Any legal source of income, including support, welfare, social security, and other benefits, must be fairly considered in evaluating a credit application, so long as the applicant can show that this income is received regularly.

New Protections for Homemakers?

To an extent, the laws of marriage are also changing to reflect more fairly the value of women's homemaking and childrearing roles. The concept of valuing a woman's domestic contributions to her family, discussed earlier in the *DiFlorido* case, may lead to new legislation to protect the homemaker against economic disaster if her marriage ends prematurely in separation, divorce, or the death of a spouse who has been the primary wage earner. Among the ideas which have been either proposed or implemented are "divorce insurance," direct coverage for homemakers under Social Security, and the setting aside of public funds to help train displaced homemakers who are making the transition into the job market.

In the employment area, much remains to be done to reverse practices which penalize women for being child bearers. In addition to the issue of employment benefits being denied to women at the time of pregnancy and childbirth, an area of increasing concern is that of occupational health and safety for women who are of childbearing age. As evidence accumulates to show that elements in certain industrial environments may be harmful to the human reproductive system, the response of some employers has been to lay off women of childbearing age. At present, Title VII forbids this type of sex discriminatory treatment. The larger question of social policy remains, however: should we force women to bear the risk of harm to their future children in order to earn a living wage, or should we insist on work environments which are safe for all people, despite the high cost of doing so?

From "Man's World" to Humane World

Similar questions arise concerning the responsibility of private and public employers to accommodate the special needs of working mothers who also shoulder the demands of raising children. A few employers have started to provide day-care facilities, more flexible working hours, job sharing, and other innovative arrangements to assist parents who work. At present, these programs are rare. Men, as well as women, stand to gain from these and other efforts to humanize the work environment and make it more compatible with family life.

Achieving the goal of sex equality will demand more than opening up an equal place for women in today's world, because it is in many ways still a "man's world." True equality for both men and women will have to encompass changes in "man's world" itself. Only then will all individuals be free to make fundamental choices and exercise control over their lives in an atmosphere of human equality.

Notes

Introduction

1. Reprinted in Alice S. Rossi, ed., *The Feminist Papers: From Adams to De Beauvoir* (New York: Bantam, 1974), pp. 10–11.

2. Reprinted in Aileen S. Kraditor, ed., *Up from the Pedestal* (Chicago: Quadrangle, 1970), pp. 184–86.

One:
Women and the Constitution

1. Bradwell v. Illinois, 38 U.S. (16 Wall) 130, 141–142 (1873) (Bradley, J., concurring).

2. United States of America v. Susan B. Anthony, 24 F. Cas. 829 (N.D.N.Y. 1873).

3. Barbara Allen Babcock, Ann E. Freedman, Eleanor Holmes Norton, and Susan C. Ross, *Sex Discrimination and the Law: Causes and Remedies* (Boston: Little, Brown, 1975), pp. 9–10.

4. Remarks of Senator George G. Vest, *Congressional Record*, 49th Cong., 2d Sess., January 25, 1887, vol. 18, p. 986.

5. Reprinted in Kraditor, *Up from the Pedestal*, p. 217.

6. Ibid., pp. 218–19.

7. Muller v. Oregon, 208 U.S. 412, 421–422, 28 S.Ct. 324, 326–327 (1908).

8. 404 U.S. 71, 92 S.Ct. 251 (1971).

9. 411 U.S. 677, 93 S.Ct. 1764 (1973).

10. 415 U.S. 912, 94 S.Ct. 1405 (1975).

11. Rostker v. Goldberg, 453 U.S. 57, 101 S. Ct. 2646 (1981).

12. Roberts v. U.S. Jaycees, _____ U.S. _____, 104 S. Ct. 3244 (1984).

Two:
Marriage and the Law

1. W. Blackstone, *Commentaries on the Laws of England* 442 (Cooley ed., 1884).

2. United States v. Yazell, 382 U.S. 341, 361, 86 S.Ct. 500,510 (1966) (Black, J., dissenting).

3. 133 N.J.Super. 403, 337 A.2d 46 (1975).

4. Blanche Crozier, "Marital Property," 15 B.U. L. REV. 28, 38 (1935).

5. McGuire v. McGuire, 157 Neb. 226, 238, 59 N.W.2d 336, 342 (1953).

6. Hardy v. Hardy, 235 F.Supp. 208, 211 (D.D.C. 1964).

7. Glover v. Glover, 64 Misc.2d 374, 375–376, 314 N.Y.S.2d 873 (1970).

8. Reprinted in Kraditor, *Up from the Pedestal,* pp. 149–50.

9. Ibid., p. 148.

10. Marya Mannes and Norman Sheresky, "A Radical Guide to Wedlock," *Saturday Review,* July 29, 1972, p. 33.

11. 459 Pa. 641, 331 A.2d 174 (1975).

Three:
Women and Employment

1. Muller v. Oregon, 208 U.S. 412, 28 S.Ct. 324 (1908).

2. Lochner v. New York, 198 U.S. 45, 25 S.Ct. 539 (1905).

3. Goesaert v. Cleary, 335 U.S. 464, 69 S.Ct. 198 (1948).

4. 29 U.S.C.A. Sec. 206.

5. 42 U.S.C.A. Sec. 2000e-5.

6. Diaz v. Pan American World Airways, Inc., 422 F.2d 385 (5th Cir., 1971).

7. Dothard v. Rawlinson, 453 U.S. 321, 97 S. Ct. 2720 (1977).

8. Hishon v. King and Spaulding, _____ U.S. _____, 104 S. Ct. 2229 (1984).

9. 438 U.S. 265, 98 S. Ct. 2733 (1978).

10. United Steelworkers of America v. Weber, 443 U.S. 193, 99 S. Ct. 2721 (1979).

11. Memphis Firefighters v. Stotts, _____ U.S. _____, 104 S. Ct. 2576 (1984).

12. U.S. Bureau of the Census, *Money Income of Households, Families, and Persons in the United States:* 1981, *Current Population Reports,* Series P-60, No. 137.

13. See e.g. AFSCME v. State of Washington, 578 F. Supp. 846 (1983), which is under appeal.

14. General Electric v. Gilbert, 429 U.S. 125, 97 S. Ct. 401 (1976).

15. City of Los Angeles Department of Water and Power v. Manhart, 435 U.S. 702, 98 S. Ct. 1370 (1978); Arizona Governing Committee v. Norris, _____ U.S. _____, 103 S. Ct. 3492 (1983).

Four:
Women and Their Bodies

1. Susan Brownmiller, *Against Our Wills: Men, Women, and Rape* (New York: Bantam, 1975), p. 16.

2. Comment, 118 U. PA. L. REV. 458, 459–60 (1970).

3. Coker v. Georgia, _____ U.S. _____, 97 S.Ct. 2861 (1977).

4. Margaret Sanger, *An Autobiography* (New York: Dover, 1971), p. 286.

5. Griswold v. Connecticut, 381 U.S. 479, 85 S.Ct. 1678 (1965).

6. Eisenstadt v. Baird, 405 U.S. 438, 92 S.Ct. 1029 (1972).

7. 410 U.S. 113, 93 S.Ct. 705 (1973).

8. 410 U.S. 179, 93 S.Ct. 739 (1973).

9. Danforth v. Planned Parenthood of Central Missouri, 428 U.S. 52, 96 S. Ct. 2831 (1976); Akron v. Akron Center for Reproductive Health, _____ U.S. _____, 103 S. Ct. 2481 (1984).

10. Beal v. Doe, 432 U.S. 438, 97 S. Ct. 2394 at 2399 (1977). See also Harris v. McRae, 448 U.S. 297, 100 S. Ct. 2671 (1980).

11. Beal v. Doe, 97 S.Ct. at 2399.

12. American Booksellers Association, Inc. v. Hudnut (Nov. 19, 1984, U.S.D.Ct., S.D. Ind.).

About the Authors

DURING THE TIME this book was written, Susan Cary Nicholas and Alice M. Price were attorneys with the Women's Law Project in Philadelphia, Pennsylvania, and Rachel Rubin was program coordinator for the Project. The Project is a nonprofit feminist law office dedicated to achieving legal equality for women through litigation, public education, research, and writing. Its in-depth study, *Women's Rights and the Law: The Impact of the ERA on State Laws*, was published in 1977. More recently, the Project has focused through education and litigation on legal remedies for sex discrimination in the fields of housing and credit. The Project also serves as a clearinghouse of information on women's legal rights for laywers, researchers, and women in need of legal assistance, and provides technical assistance to governmental agencies on matters of concern to women.

A Note on Language

IN EDITING BOOKS, The Feminist Press attempts to eliminate harmful sex and race bias inherent in the language. In order to retain the authenticity of historical and literary documents, however, our policy is to leave their original language unaltered. We recognize that the task of changing language usage is extremely complex and that it will not be easily accomplished. The process is an ongoing one that we share with many others concerned with the relationship between a humane language and a more humane world.

Index

The Feminist Press at the City University of New York offers alternatives in education and in literature. Founded in 1970, this non-profit, tax-exempt educational and publishing organization works to eliminate sexual stereotypes in books and schools and to provide literature with a broad vision of human potential. The publishing program includes reprints of important works by women, feminist biographies of women, and nonsexist children's books. Curricular materials, bibliographies, directories, and a quarterly journal provide information and support for students and teachers of women's studies. In-service projects help to transform teaching methods and curricula. Through publications and projects, The Feminist Press contributes to the rediscovery of the history of women and the emergence of a more humane society.

FEMINIST CLASSICS FROM THE FEMINIST PRESS

Antoinette Brown Blackwell: A Biography, by Elizabeth Cazden. $19.95 cloth, $9.95 paper.
Between Mothers and Daughters: Stories Across a Generation. Edited by Susan Koppelman. $8.95 paper.
Brown Girl, Brownstones, a novel by Paule Marshall. Afterword by Mary Helen Washington. $8.95 paper.
Call Home the Heart, a novel of the thirties, by Fielding Burke. Introduction by Alice Kessler-Harris and Paul Lauter and afterwords by Sylvia J. Cook and Anna W. Shannon. $8.95 paper.
Cassandra, by Florence Nightingale. Introduction by Myra Stark. Epilogue by Cynthia Macdonald. $3.50 paper.
The Changelings, a novel by Jo Sinclair. Afterwords by Nellie McKay; and by Johnnetta B. Cole and Elizabeth H. Oakes; biographical note by Elisabeth Sandberg. $8.95 paper.
The Convert, a novel by Elizabeth Robins. Introduction by Jane Marcus. $6.95 paper.
Daughter of Earth, a novel by Agnes Smedley. Afterword by Paul Lauter. $7.95 paper.
A Day at a Time: The Diary Literature of American Women from 1764 to the Present, edited and with an introduction by Margo Culley. $29.95 cloth, $12.95 paper.
The Defiant Muse: French Feminist Poems from the Middle Ages to the Present, a bilingual anthology edited and with an introduction by Domna C. Stanton. $29.95 cloth, $11.95 paper.
The Defiant Muse: German Feminist Poems from the Middle Ages to the Present, a bilingual anthology edited and with an introduction by Susan L. Cocalis. $29.95 cloth, $11.95 paper.
The Defiant Muse: Hispanic Feminist Poems from the Middle Ages to the Present, a bilingual anthology edited and with an introduction by Angel Flores and Kate Flores. $29.95 cloth, $11.95 paper.
The Defiant Muse: Italian Feminist Poems from the Middle Ages to the Present, a bilingual anthology edited by Beverly Allen, Muriel Kittel, and Keala Jane Jewell, and with an introduction by Beverly Allen. $29.95 cloth, $11.95 paper.
The Female Spectator, edited by Mary R. Mahl and Helene Koon. $8.95 paper.
Guardian Angel and Other Stories, by Margery Latimer. Afterwords by Nancy Loughridge, Meridel Le Sueur, and Louis Kampf. $8.95 paper.
I Love Myself When I Am Laughing...And Then Again When I Am Looking Mean and Impressive, by Zora Neale Hurston. Edited by Alice Walker with an introduction by Mary Helen Washington. $9.95 paper.
Käthe Kollwitz: Woman and Artist, by Martha Kearns. $7.95 paper.
Life in the Iron Mills and Other Stories, by Rebecca Harding Davis. Biographical interpretation by Tillie Olsen. $7.95 paper.
The Living Is Easy, a novel by Dorothy West. Afterword by Adelaide M. Cromwell. $8.95 paper.
The Other Woman: Stories of Two Women and a Man. Edited by Susan Koppelman. $8.95 paper.
Mother to Daughter, Daughter to Mother: A Daybook and Reader, selected and shaped by Tillie Olsen. $9.95 paper.

Portraits of Chinese Women in Revolution, by Agnes Smedley. Edited with an introduction by Jan MacKinnon and Steve MacKinnon and an afterword by Florence Howe. $5.95 paper.
Reena and Other Stories, selected short stories by Paule Marshall. $8.95 paper.
Ripening: Selected Work, 1927–1980, by Meridel Le Sueur. Edited with an introduction by Elaine Hedges. $8.95 paper.
Rope of Gold, a novel of the thirties, by Josephine Herbst. Introduction by Alice Kessler-Harris and Paul Lauter and afterword by Elinor Langer. $8.95 paper.
The Silent Partner, a novel by Elizabeth Stuart Phelps. Afterword by Mari Jo Buhle and Florence Howe. $8.95.
Swastika Night, a novel by Katharine Burdekin. Introduction by Daphne Patai. $8.95 paper.
These Modern Women: Autobiographical Essays from the Twenties. Edited with an introduction by Elaine Showalter. $4.95 paper.
The Unpossessed, a novel of the thirties, by Tess Slesinger. Introduction by Alice Kessler-Harris and Paul Lauter and afterword by Janet Sharistanian. $8.95 paper.
Weeds, a novel by Edith Summers Kelley. Afterword by Charlotte Goodman. $7.95 paper.
A Woman of Genius, a novel by Mary Austin. Afterword by Nancy Porter. $8.95 paper.
The Woman and the Myth: Margaret Fuller's Life and Writings, by Bell Gale Chevigny. $8.95 paper.
Women and Appletrees, a novel by Moa Martinson. Translated from the Swedish and with an afterword by Margaret S. Lacy. $8.95 paper.
The Yellow Wallpaper, by Charlotte Perkins Gilman. Afterword by Elaine Hedges. $4.50 paper.

OTHER TITLES FROM THE FEMINIST PRESS

Black Foremothers: Three Lives, by Dorothy Sterling. $8.95 paper.
All The Women Are White, All The Blacks Are Men, But Some of Us Are Brave: Black Women's Studies. Edited by Gloria T. Hull, Patricia Bell Scott, and Barbara Smith. $12.95.
Complaints and Disorders: The Sexual Politics of Sickness, by Barbara Ehrenreich and Deirdre English. $3.95 paper.
The Cross-Cultural Study of Women. Edited by Margot I. Duley and Mary I. Edwards. $29.95 cloth, $12.95 paper.
Feminist Resources for Schools and Colleges: A Guide to Curricular Materials., 3rd edition. Compiled and edited by Anne Chapman. $12.95 paper.
Household and Kin: Families in Flux, by Amy Swerdlow et al. $8.95 paper.
How to Get Money for Research, by Mary Rubin and the Business and Professional Women's Foundation. Foreword by Mariam Chamberlain. $6.95 paper.
In Her Own Image: Women Working in the Arts. Edited with an introduction by Elaine Hedges and Ingrid Wendt. $9.95 paper.
Integrating Women's Studies into the Curriculum: A Guide and Bibliography, by Betty Schmitz. $9.95 paper.
Las Mujeres: Conversations from a Hispanic Community, by Nan Elsasser, Kyle MacKenzie, and Yvonne Tixier y Vigil. $8.95 paper.
Lesbian Studies: Present and Future. Edited by Margaret Cruikshank. $9.95 paper.
Moving the Mountain: Women Working for Social Change, by Ellen Cantarow with Susan Gushee O'Malley and Sharon Hartman Strom. $8.95 paper.
Out of the Bleachers: Writings on Women and Sport. Edited with an introduction by Stephanie L. Twin. $9.95 paper.
Reconstructing American Literature: Courses, Syllabi, Issues. Edited by Paul Lauter. $10.95 paper.
Salt of the Earth, screenplay by Michael Wilson with historical commentary by Deborah Silverton Rosenfelt. $5.95 paper.
Witches, Midwives, and Nurses: A History of Women Healers, by Barbara Ehrenreich and Deirdre English. $3.95 paper.

With These Hands: Women Working on the Land. Edited with an introduction by Joan M. Jensen. $9.95 paper.

Woman's "True" Profession: Voices from the History of Teaching. Edited with an introduction by Nancy Hoffman. $9.95 paper.

Women Have Always Worked: A Historical Overview, by Alice Kessler-Harris. $8.95 paper.

Women Working: An Anthology of Stories and Poems. Edited and with an introduction by Nancy Hoffman and Florence Howe. $8.95 paper.

For free catalog, write to The Feminist Press at the City University of New York, 311 East 94 Street, New York, N.Y. 10128. Send individual book orders to The Feminist Press, P.O. Box 1654, Hagerstown, MD 21741. Include $1.75 postage and handling for one book and 75¢ for each additional book. To order using MasterCard or Visa, call: (800) 638-3030.